MW01101314

I Will Not Live in Vain

By Rae M. Meadows

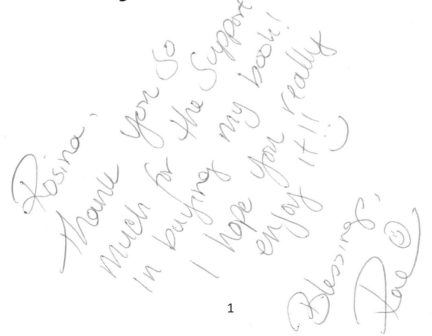

<u>Preface</u>

"What if a demon were to creep after you one night, in your loneliest loneliness, and say, 'This life which you live must be lived by you once again and innumerable times more; and every pain and joy and thought and sigh must come again to you, all in the same sequence. The eternal hourglass will again and again be turned and you with it, dust of the dust!' Would you throw yourself down and gnash your teeth and curse that demon? Or would you answer, 'Never have I heard anything more divine'?"

&*Friedrich Nietzsche*

I wonder if I write a book, would anyone read it? Would my life laid out in the pages of a paperback, or the screen of a kindle be of any interest to the masses? Would only my children read it? My father led what sounds like an amazing life before I was born. Even after my sisters and I came around, his life was pretty cool. But often in my life, my dad would reference something about himself from prior to us and we would exclaim something to the effect of "What? You never told us that!" He would simply reply "Well, you never asked." How would we know to ask such things as "Did you live in Vietnam when you were fourteen?" or "Dad, did you ever learn Thai?" I only learned that my dad had briefly been married before my mum after I had moved out of the house! How was I to know to ask that, I wonder?

I decided to start going through my life experiences and start writing them down, in book form, so at the very least my children will know me – know me more than just "mum." That they may pass on tidbits about me to my grandchildren once I am gone. Though this particular version has all names changed, including family members in some capacity.

I am Rae Meadows. Currently, I am married to a man named Jason and we have two children – one girl and one boy. At this point in my life, I am thirty-one years old. I imagine it will take me a long time to record thirty-one years onto paper, but God willing, I will have many more years ahead of me to work on this and leave a legacy of some sort. I hope that I will be able to express some of what I want to pass down to my kids; to my daughter I want to impart my experiences as I get into older years and deal with growing up as a female character lead in my own story. I want her to know how to handle social relationships, especially the relationships with men. One could hope that these areas would help my son as well – to see it from a female perspective.

Chapter 1

"Men are by nature wanderers...Every people has moved from somewhere, and had to learn the ways of the land from the people who were there before."

∾Marion Zimmer Bradley,
The Forest House

As any autobiography should start, I must say "I was born Rachel Jensson…" or "In 1983 I came into this world…" In all seriousness though, I was born in Tacoma Falls, Maryland to my parents Diane and Karl Jensson. I was born in the midst of a snowstorm – a snowstorm in which my father got stuck in his car and had to spend the night there while my mum and I were safe in the Hospital. I am unsure if having been born during a snowstorm has affected my feelings for snow… But I love it. I love the crispness of the air, that perfect chill. I love the coming inside for a warm cup of cocoa and a snuggly blanket after that chill. I am sure my dad did not feel such fondness for the snow at that time though.

When I was born, my parents actually lived in Manassas, VA. My father was a police officer for the first year of my life, then shortly afterwards he joined back up with the Air Force as a telecommunications officer. So, even though I was born in the USA, I was hardly raised there. More than half my life has been traveling around to various countries. All I knew as a kid was that I was getting to do cool things and that my dad worked for the Air Force and then later the State Department.

I don't specifically remember a lot of events from my early years, so this section may go rather quickly. It may be a bit disjointed. I think anyone's early memories come in fits and starts. So bear with me as I lay out some background information in these first few chapters. A lot of what I used to think I remembered I later discovered was on home video, so I likely was just remembering seeing the videos from a young age.

When I was about three years old, we moved to Djibouti in Africa. I remember desert and I remember chasing camels. Well, there is a home video of myself chasing camels in the desert. The perfect example of what I thought I remembered, but was actually a video.

One memory I do have from this time was a preschool memory. I remember I was supposed to colour a turtle. God knows why it was so important for us to colour a turtle, but I just plain did not want to. My teacher made me stay in (all by myself) from recess. I was grumping with my arms folded as kids do when I looked at the crayons and thought about the boy in my class that always got in trouble for eating them. I thought to myself "Well, if he likes them... maybe..." My thoughts then quickly turned to "ACK! That kid is CRAZY!" Up to that point crayons were probably the nastiest thing I had ever tried to eat. Shortly after that, I just coloured the dang picture so I could go out and play. In my memory it feels like I held out for a long, valiant effort of a time – but logically I know my three year old self probably didn't last five minutes.

We only lived in Djibouti for a year or so, as it was considered a hardship post. My mum told me of young Marines that would commit suicide while stationed there in the 1980s. I don't know what made it so difficult for adults – but as a three year old I enjoyed my time there. We lived on a little compound and I imagine that is where I spent most of my time. I also didn't fully grasp the poverty that I would see when I ventured away from the house with my parents. I do have one other memory from then... I remember being mad at my parents and I decided to run away. I packed a little satchel and hung it off of a stick just like I saw in cartoons and ran away – to the bush back behind the house. Obviously I couldn't get far with a gate and a guard blocking my exit, so the bush had to do. That is, until I eventually got hungry and went back inside.

After we left Djibouti, we moved back to Virginia for a short time. I attended Fresta Valley Christian School for preschool. I had Mrs Ashland as my teacher, and I believe Mrs O'Grady as the teacher assistant. The only reason I remember those specifics is that Fresta Valley was where I went back and attended for 7th grade and 8th grade. One main thing that I remember from preschool there – and the beginning of my formative events that shaped my current Christian views – was that daily we would have prayer time. During this prayer time we would have to sit perfectly still, with our eyes closed, the lights would be off, and the prayer time at least seemed to last forever. Invariably, I would usually get uncomfortable and shift in my seat – and no matter how slightly I moved, it would mean no "Good Job" type ribbon that they handed out afterwards. I don't know how often I was actually successful in gaining one of these coveted ribbons, but I only recall getting it once, maybe twice. Of course it was very exciting, and I was so proud of myself when I got it. But then nearly every day I would feel like a failure when I didn't get it. Even now I feel like Mrs Ashland had too high an expectation for four year olds.

While living in Virginia this time around I suddenly was no longer an only child. My sister, Sarah Leigh, was born in 1986 in the same hospital I was born in. She was also born in winter time, but there was no snowstorm – so I guess I still had her beat. I should probably say something about how losing the only child status affected me, but I don't recall worrying too much about that. I remember visiting mum in the hospital and peering at my new sister through the nursery window, trying to figure out which one was ours.

Around 1987 we moved to England. England is a beautiful, but often dreary country. Dreary because of the usual clouds and rain, but I tend to prefer a bit of dreariness to my weather. England is also full of lush countryside and quaint old cottages. My memories start to become more consistent from this age as by this time I was of school age.

We lived on an Air Force base near Oxford, but I did not attend a DoD school. My parents had the view of wanting their kids to get as fully immersed in other cultures as was appropriate and beneficial, while still teaching US heritage at home. I attended Beachborough private school off base. Beachborough was a large old private boarding school. It looked much like any stereotypical British boarding school set in the countryside, as seen in many movies. Even though it was a boarding school, I lived close enough that I did not board there myself. From what I remember, it was a great school. We wore pretty little pinafore dresses, grey and blue, cardigans, everything that makes a British school British. We did swimming, ballet, and tap dance as part of our curriculum. I even remember having recorder class – believe it or not I still remember how to play "hot cross buns" ha ha! We had special coveralls we would wear over our uniforms during recess so as not to dirty them. My teacher's name was Mrs Hillmann. I remember being so proud when I finally spelled her name correctly. Just as proud as when I finally remembered my middle name was spelled "Megan" not "Magen."

I remember this huge school had large class tables that we'd sit at for lunch. The meal being served up by a teacher at each table. Here I learned about the 'proper' way to hold a knife and fork. I also acquired a taste for spaghetti Bolognese, rhubarb pie, and – much to my parent's revulsion – Brussel sprouts. Also at this school, I was instructed to hold my pencil a certain way in a certain hand. I used to be a bit ambidextrous, but I lost that when they made me use my right hand. I never did have a lasting habit of holding the pencil the 'proper' way as it hurt my hand to do so. I never got used to it – so as soon as I left that school I went back to my natural way of doing it.

My parents also giggled not necessarily that I developed a British accent, but moreover that the school taught us to sing "Deep in the Heart of Texas" for some reason, and as we all sung it for the parents our British accents were all the more noticeable.

While in England in 1988, our family became five as my next sister, Esther Kirsten, was born. She was our token foreign kid for a while, but sooner or later that title would be taken from her when our last sister was born.

Our base was surrounded by farm land. Once in a while we kids from the base would crawl under the bushes, through gaps in the fence, to play in the fields. The farmer, of course, was not pleased when we did. One field had hay bales to climb, but my favourite was the one with poppies. Naturally we *had* to run through it saying "Poppies! Poppies! Poppies!" as if we were in the *Wizard of Oz*. There was actually a lot of farmland around the area, and I remember going on hikes with my dad through large fields and climbing over wooden fences.

A few notable memories from England are that dad was an extra in the *Indiana Jones and the Last Crusade* movie. He was a Nazi extra in the book burning scene and it was filmed at my swim school. I'm not sure if this was my dad's first acting job, or if it was just the first I knew of, but when I was a teenager he also did several commercials, a music video, a film festival movie, and was the face for a comedic book character… all sorts that I will go into later, but I always thought it was so cool to see my dad on screen.

Another big event in my life was when I cracked my head open and had to get eight stitches. My mum had dropped us off at a day care like centre on base while she went shopping or something like that; my dad was working night shift so he was sleeping. From what I remember we went there fairly often, but not all the time. At least I knew these people. I remember at this age (about six years old) I *hated* my name. I thought I wanted a prettier name, so whenever my mum would drop me off at this place I would tell them my name was "Crystal" or "Ruby" or something like that. I thought that since they were also names of jewels, and jewels are pretty, that made them pretty names. I know, I know… but I was six years old. Let's not forget that. Whenever I would go and my mum would sign me in, they'd ask me what my name was that day.

This centre had large cement blocks that were painted to look like ABC blocks. For some reason this day they allowed me and some friends to jump and run across the top of them. As I was jumping from one to the other, back and forth, I miss-stepped and fell in between two, smacking my forehead and the blood started to gush. The next memory is of lying in the back of a car with a teacher holding a towel to my head. In the hospital I noticed blood on my shoes - my favourite blue sneakers. I was told that they were still trying to get a hold of my dad. As he was sleeping he had taken the phone off of the hook. Back then there was no such thing as cell phones, so they couldn't ring my mum. I remember looking up at the lights and then they put a surgical cloth over my face and stitched me up. It felt really weird. At that time they were still using the kind of thread that had to be removed at a later date. Right about the time they started, our next door neighbour arrived to hold my hand through it. They had successfully gotten a hold of her and she knocked on our door until my dad woke up. He arrived shortly after the procedure was done. I remember the Doctor gave me some thread so I could sew up the forehead of one of my dolls. If I remember correctly, it was a cabbage patch doll. Then, when I went back to get the stitches out, she came with me to get hers out too.

This scar has been with me for most of my life now and at this point I usually forget that it is there. I was self-conscious for a long time about it, but by now it has faded enough that you really have to pay attention to see it. Either that or I am starting to get wrinkles that hide it...

Chapter 2

"By having good memories on every place you just visit, you are building paradise in your own heart and your life."

&Toba Beta,
Master of Stupidity

After England we moved to a small island off the coast of Madagascar in the Indian Ocean. A little island called "Mauritius." It was the home to the now extinct "Dodo" bird; it was an island with gorgeous blue water, masses of sugar cane fields, and a population of mostly French speaking Hindu people. It was exotic. It was beautiful.

I only have happy memories from this time in my life. I attended a French curriculum school called "Alexander House School." I remember running around in that school yard, I remember picking lychees from the trees and eating them with my friends. I remember my French teacher who would stop the whole class and make us count to sixty in French when someone went to the bathroom. Not sure why she did that exactly, but I do know that it means I can now pee in under a minute.

I remember our house was huge to me. Not only was the house itself spacious - Broken Hill, as it was called, also had fairly extensive grounds. On one side we had a gated fruit and vegetable garden. We had a papaya tree, a guava tree, and just outside that gate was also a banana tree. The back yard was split into two levels with a huge stone staircase going down to the bottom garden. Actually it was split in three with the most bottom level housing servants' quarters. You had to go around the side of the property to get down there.

In this garden we had three or four fountains. My parents didn't see the use in them or any reason to bother with the water and the maintaining of them so they just left them be. To me and my sisters, however; they became pirate ships. Especially the large, rectangular one in the middle of the top garden.

In Mauritius, we all got our own puppy. They were sibling pups. Mine was all white and named "Princess Snowflake." My sisters had "Lady Liquorice" and "Duchess Spot." You can guess what colours those puppies were, I'm sure. These puppies were housed in a side garden that happened to be adjacent to the large windows that went into my sisters' huge playroom bedroom. I'm sure, armed with that information, you can guess that the puppies *ahem* found their way into the house occasionally.

I had my own room and I felt so grown up. In between my room and my sisters' room was a hall area with a bathroom. This bathroom had a door with a key lock. Since my dad was very much into *Star Trek: The Next Generation* when I was a kid, naturally my sister Sarah and I would need to play that at some point. We decided this bathroom was the most "space" looking room in the house so it would be our "bridge." We locked ourselves in. We finished playing and then realized we were stuck. Years later Sarah would tell me she remembered it was near Easter time because she remembered being worried we'd miss Easter and thought we'd be stuck in there forever. Eventually my dad heard us screaming and he came to save the day. We slid the key under the door so he could unlock it and let us out.

I don't remember many other significant things from Mauritius except its extreme beauty. We had an awesome view from the house that included mountain ranges and numerous sugarcane fields, the Indian Ocean on the horizon. There was a beach house that was shared amongst people from the Embassy, so we got to do several weekend beach trips. When we first arrived, and right before leaving, we stayed at a gorgeous hotel by sparkling waters and white beaches. I remember wearing parios (called sarongs elsewhere) as I walked amongst palm trees. I hope one day I can take my kids there for a visit, just to see the beauty of it all.

<u>Chapter 3</u>

"Alone of all the races on earth, they seem to be free from the 'Grass is Greener on the other side of the fence' syndrome, and roundly proclaim that Australia is, in fact, the other side of that fence."

∞Douglas Adams

Around late 1992 or early 1993, we moved to Australia. Australia is one of the most diverse countries I have ever been to. Some areas are lush and green, others are deserts or swamps. Then there are beaches on tropical coasts. We lived smack dab in the middle of the country – the middle of desert country. Red dirt and scrub brush wouldn't sound like a beautiful scene to most people, but this area is actually quite lovely. The way the red dirt and majestic red mountains seem to change colour in varying degrees of light and the multi-coloured birds congregating on fields or in the trees.

We arrived in the Red Centre (Alice Springs) after a stop-over in Adelaide where we stayed for a few days to find a car, as there weren't many options to buy in Alice. My last sister, Havilah Kylie, was born in Alice Springs, exactly ten years and six days after me.

I started out by attending Araluen Christian School. I have fond memories from then. My teacher, Mr Davison, taught me for 5th and 6th grade in this small school. I remember him in his shorts and knee high socks. I remember his guitar. I remember him taking us for hikes in the bush surrounding the school grounds and I remember exploring caves. I remember once he showed us how to make damper bread in the ground out there.

I met a few good friends, including another American girl named Jennifer. I remember playing with Barbies at her house and her dad exclaiming he had "never seen so many naked women in [his] life" when he saw the pile of undressed dolls. That still makes me laugh to think about. I also remember her mum teaching us how to dance hula, and then doing a performance of it in town.

At the time, Araluen only went up to 6th grade. So in 1995 I went on to start St Philips College for 7th grade. Australian schools do the calendar year schedule for school, so I actually only did half a year there because in

June or July that year we moved back to the US and I had to restart 7th grade in September in order to get the whole school year finished.

I enjoyed my time at St Philips, though I expect I was a bit of a punk. I was at a point that I thought I was tough, and was a bit tomboyish, so I'd end up butting heads with boys I had actually liked. One particular guy that stands out in my memory was John. I remember as well his friend Rhys had tried to flirt with me when I first started and I pushed him. From then on out it became Rhys' mission to harass me. John actually said something nice to me when we first met. He said something nice about my hair if I remember correctly. I distrusted that he was sincere and I shot him a dirty look. Over the months we ended up fighting a bit and flirting in that immature "I hate you, but I actually secretly like you" kind of way. Ah, kids in love. Well, at least I was.

I now work with someone who attended school with me that same year – except that he was in 11th grade. He tells me that he and his friends would keep a watch over the "little ones" and that he remembers me because I was one of the little ones. So much for me thinking I was so tough.

ೞೞ

In Australia I got to have several fun experiences. I saw Ayers Rock and, because I am a sissy, only climbed up the first part of the rock before getting back down. Dad made it to the top though. I got to ride camels. I went on a cruise on the P&O Fairstar around New Zealand. I did not do well on the cruise itself as far as not throwing up from sea sickness, but it was still fun. I remember the pizza place on board. Best pizza I ever had, and I don't know that I've ever found another slice quite as good as that. During stop offs on shore we got to experience things like the Glow Worm cave. We also took a trip to Sydney, and at one point I went to a nice ranch to spend a weekend with my mum.

I also did Girl Guides and became a patrol leader. It was a natural step to join in with them as I had started Bluebirds (the Mauritian name for Brownies) before I had come. I learned a lot through this organization,

16

and I am pleased that now that my daughter is five she has decided she wants to do Girl Guides here in Australia again.

For a long time Australia was at the top of my favourite places list, and in 1995 when it was time to leave, I was sad to see it go.

Chapter 4

"I cannot fix on the hour, or the spot, or the look or the words, which laid the foundation. It is too long ago. I was in the middle before I knew that I had begun."

ᴐJane Austen,
Pride and Prejudice

After we left Australia, we moved back to the US for a couple of years. We went back to Virginia, and I went back to Fresta Valley Christian School. We lived in a different town this time, however; and Fresta Valley was a good forty-five minute drive from our house that was nestled in the Shenandoah Mountains in the small town of Front Royal.

Fresta Valley was stifling to me. I made a fair few friends at this school, but it was a repressive atmosphere. I remember one day the school called my parents to tell them that Friday would be a casual dress day. To any normal person casual dress would mean what? Jeans? A T-shirt? Well, that's what I thought anyway.

I showed up to school realizing that every other kid was wearing nice clothes. Nice in the respect that the boys were still wearing ties. It was much too late for my parents to take me home, as they had to get to work as well. My embarrassment was made worse by the embarrassed-for-me look that the principal wore when she saw me. She told me that we were supposed to wear "church clothes" to casual day. I looked her in the eye, not understanding. I said "These are my church clothes."

My mum had to take me out that weekend to buy a bunch of "church clothes" because I otherwise didn't own anything that fit the bill.

It bothered me when on a slightly drizzly day the girls had to stay in from PE to bake cookies. One day we did quilting. The boys still got to go outside to play soccer. The girls forfeited their only outside time those days because it was slightly chilly or there was a threat of rain.

They would go through our lockers and would have a list of kids that would have to clean their lockers by the end of the day. Fair enough, I guess (we did have a few kids attracting fruit flies after all), but one day they called my parents in for a meeting because I had a secular looking picture in my locker, worse yet others could see it when I opened the door. The picture in question was a group of friends of mine that were in a Christian band. They were performing at Fishnet festival, a Christian music festival that my church put on annually. But they didn't look Christian. I guess I didn't look Christian away from school either.

I had some good friends at that school, but I didn't feel like I fit in there at all. I felt judged. There were kids expelled for meaningless things. I desperately wanted to attend public school, but the one in Front Royal had a bad reputation, so I was stuck where I was. Later my dad confessed that he wasn't happy with Fresta Valley and that he hated the way the principal, Mrs Blumberg, would talk down to him. But it was better than sending me to Warren High.

Chapter 5

"Wake me up when it's all over, when I'm wiser and I'm older. All this time I was finding myself and I, I didn't know I was lost."

&Avicii
Wake Me Up

Most of the foundation of what I believe affected my relationships was laid while I lived in Virginia as a middle schooler. I met Wyatt at Fishnet church in Front Royal where we both lived. At the beginning, Fishnet was still in a storefront on Main Street, though they had a large lot of land that they had been holding festivals at for decades. Eventually while attending there, they built a big, new building at that site.

While at this church, though I feared hell and believed in God, most of my faith was more of a lip service. I acted the part, and I showed up to Youth Group. On Sundays I danced on the dance team, but inwardly I really just went for my friends.

I met Wyatt while the youth met at the storefront. I don't remember exactly how our first meeting went, or how it came to be that we were in a relationship. I was only almost fourteen at the time; Wyatt was an older boy – turning sixteen shortly after we started dating. I don't know what attracted me to him, besides I thought he was cool as a skater boy and, of course, he was an older, *mature*, guy that was interested in *me*!

I look back at my younger self, and I realize that I was thin and beautiful – yet I didn't really seem to realize it as fact. Over the years, I would wonder why someone was flirting with me, and was insecure when someone I liked didn't seem to like me. I am unsure when exactly this insecurity started. I honestly don't know if it had started before Wyatt, or if it was created and exacerbated by my relationship with him.

I remember much later, sometime around the age seventeen, I went on a date with a man named Dan, as I sat down across from him at this busy little cafe he asked me what was going through my head. I decided to be bold, as that was something I worked on making myself do, and I told him the truth. "I'm just feeling intimidated right now." He looked up, surprised, he asked me why. "When I was younger, I had relationship with an older boy. He was controlling, and it damaged my confidence when it comes to men." Simple, and to the point. He accepted that answer, and I

22

don't know that he would have been comfortable to hear much more. Danny was a few years older than me as well – he was nineteen at that point. But he is a story for another chapter.

My relationship with Wyatt started out innocent enough. We met at church, after all. He was well liked, was a skater boy, but also a football player. I fell easily into his group of friends. I'm not sure what they thought at the time about Wyatt dating such a young girl. Not that the age difference was all that large – but in high school, dating a middle schooler could seem like a huge gap. But they accepted me, nonetheless, after all - I was Wyatt's girl.

I was allowed to hang with his friends because when I did, he was there as well. Or if he wasn't, it was only the females I hung out with away from him – and they were mostly kids from our church. I think it must have been a saving grace that I attended a school in a different county. Wyatt did not know anyone from my school.

As mentioned, I went to Fresta Valley. It was a small school with 7th and 8th grades in the same class, the second year of which they added High School and all of those students also fit in one class room. Because it was such a small school, almost everybody in the class were friends of some sort. No way you could avoid anyone in any case. My mistake was saying anything.

I had a good friend named Adam at school. He was cool, I thought. He was also my age – but at that time I hadn't developed any feelings for him. I was so convinced of my devotion to Wyatt. Everyone at school knew of my boyfriend and how in love we were. I don't remember what I said. All I know is I said the wrong thing.

As I sat with Wyatt in his bedroom, we were talking about school – just chatting, nothing special. I decided to tell him some amusing anecdote; some event that had happened. I don't remember now what it was. What I do remember is that I used Adam's name in reference to this event.

Suddenly, my cheek was stinging. I realized Wyatt had slapped me across the face. I realized this because I looked down and his hand was clutched around my left bicep.

"What..." I started to ask what was happening.

Wyatt cut me off. "I knew it! I knew you were cheating on me, you slut! Who is this Adam?!" He sneered at me.

"Uh, nobody...Nobody... I swear! Just a guy at school... Wyatt! You're hurting me!" Stumbling over my words, I grabbed at his hand trying to wrench his fingers off of me.

He released my arm.

"I'm not cheating on you. Baby, I swear, I'm not cheating on you," a single tear threatening to fall from my lashes.

He sighed, unclenching his fist.

"I just love you so much," he said, "the thought of you with other guys..." trailing off.

"I..."

He snapped back to attention. "Promise me you won't speak to Adam again."

I knew this was unreasonable. How could I explain not talking to Adam again? Not like I could avoid him in our school, small as it was. But what was I to do? I considered it quickly, I loved Wyatt, he loved me – "I just want him to be happy," I thought.

"Of course, If that's what you want, Wyatt. I won't talk to Adam again."

"I don't want you talking to any guy at school." He said sternly.

"Oh... Uh, okay." I agreed.

The next morning as I got dressed I noticed the finger shaped bruises on my arm.

Later that day, my mum said that Wyatt's mum told her that he had been so sad the previous night after I left, because I had "teased" him about other boys. My mum advised me to be nice to Wyatt and not hurt his feelings anymore.

I didn't tell Adam, or anyone, about Wyatt's decree. I resolved to keep my mouth shut about school when talking to Wyatt. Even in love as I was, I knew it was unreasonable to "not talk" to any of the boys at school. Luckily my school was far enough away that Wyatt didn't know any of my classmates.

ഇരുജ

Despite my efforts, I still seemed to make him angry and jealous sometimes. If we were anywhere where there were people nearby, I would be able to tell that he was angry by the way he would stiffen and clench his fist, but he wouldn't act on the anger in those cases and it would have usually worn off by the time we were alone. I suppose it was this reason that I felt more comfortable teasing him when we were near other people, just because I could. Not that the teasing I did would have been considered out of line in any normal relationship. But if we were alone when he got angry with me I would sometimes get slapped again, but most often my wrists were grabbed, pulling me up towards him – trapping me – as he screamed in my face. Most often he was angry for thinking I was unfaithful so words such as "slut" and "whore" were thrown around liberally.

He always apologized after his outbursts, and as a wiser woman now I know that did not make it okay. As a fourteen year old, however; I took it as a sign of his love, and of my fault for angering him.

I want my daughter to know that being sweet and loving the rest of the time still does not excuse this kind of behaviour. I never want my daughter to feel the way that I did.

25

ഇരു

I'm not sure when it started, but the love of my life at that point also introduced me to my sexuality. I was much too young and not nearly emotionally ready enough for such acts, but yet there I was, with my older boy. I had enough fear of God in me that I held off on the actual intercourse, no matter how much he requested it and claimed he loved me. Yet, he convinced me of just about everything else. He said if I loved him, I would do it. I was afraid of making him angry again. He liked to leave marks on me that looking back now seems like he was marking his territory. He would give me what he called "hickeys" usually on my chest, occasionally on my abdomen – but further experience made me realize that hickeys did not have to hurt like his did. He basically just bit me, leaving large bruises. When they would start to fade he would comment on it, and put fresh ones on me. These bruises would be easily hidden from my parents, but not so well hidden from the girls at school in the change room. By the time they were noticed by another girl in the change room, however; I had forgotten to even attempt to hide them. They had been there so long. I acted nonchalant and proud of my *promiscuity*. It meant somebody wanted me.

He had ways of making me feel as though I was his and his alone. The overall thought of this made me feel wanted, though I continually felt under his control as well. I remembered that first slap and the bruises on my arm. I did not want to anger him. I was naïve enough to think I was in love, that this is how relationships must work. I naïvely believed that he loved me just as much as he said he did. After all, he had such strong feelings about me, as he had displayed previously.

He said he loved me, he said he wanted to marry me. He gave me a ring. When he was in a good mood, I was called "Baby Doll," as in his sweet plaything. I thought that meant it was okay to do what we did. Looking back I see his manipulation. I see the girls he cheated on me with – the girls that were his age and gave in to sex. The girls he forbade me to talk with when they showed up to some church youth events. The girls for which I forgave him.

26

In 1997, my family was to move to Ethiopia. I was devastated. Wyatt was devastated. He came up with a plan to run off together.

A few days before my family was to leave, we went to stay in a hotel. My friend, Callie, came to stay in a room with me. We watched our favourite movies: Grease and Grease 2. We took provocative swimsuit pictures, because Wyatt wanted some of me. We did all of our normal sleep over activities.

One of the days we went out to a waterpark or something. When we came back there were presents waiting: a white bear and a dozen roses lying on my bed. Wyatt had come and gotten the hotel staff to open the door so he could leave them for me. On one hand, I was bothered that the hotel would just open the room, but on the other it was such a romantic gesture. Swoon.

I can't remember if I decided running off with Wyatt wasn't a good idea, or if it was simply that he didn't have a car or the money to act on the plan, but in 1997 I left for Ethiopia – my devotion for Wyatt intact.

Chapter 6

"I am no bird; and no net ensnares me; I am a free human being, with an independent will; which I now exert to leave you."

&Charlotte Brontë,
Jane Eyre

Getting off of the plane in Addis Ababa, the first thing you notice is the smell. I don't know when I stopped noticing the smell. I don't look back on Ethiopia now thinking there was any noticeable scent, but I do remember getting off that plane, wrinkling my nose, and wondering what the hell I was doing there instead of back home, with Wyatt.

This was the first move in my life that I hadn't been excited about. I love traveling, getting to go to strange and exotic places. But in 1997, I was nearly fifteen and my friends and my boyfriend were back in the States.

Ethiopia, while having some lovely and charming aspects, was basically a pit. The westerners and the rich had many amenities but the back drop was that of an impoverished nation with barely paved roads and often dead cows and trash alongside those roads. My father said after we left that he was never going to go to Africa again. He'd been there, done that, and hated it. He told me that he would never even take a flight in which the course would cross over that continent again – for fear the plane might crash and he would die in Africa. He said if he would have to die in an airplane crash, he would hope it would be in the ocean instead.

My feelings were not that strong about Ethiopia. I certainly did not love it there, but I did not hate it that much. I had a hard time while there, but by the time I left I did not harbour the same kinds of feelings as dad had.

My dad and sisters, Sarah and Esther, had moved there a couple months ahead of time. This was an effort of my parents to let me have some extra transition time, to get that last bit of time with my friends and Wyatt. This also allowed my mum to have time to finish up some business.

When I arrived, my dad had reserved the best room in the house for me. It was an apartment like room on the roof of the house, with and external door and its own bathroom with shower. When you walked in, there was a long corridor with windows running down both sides which opened up to a large room with more windows along two walls. The house itself was three stories high and had a few large arch windows and a balcony on the front side of the second floor. Inside it was mostly marble floors and hardwood ceilings. The roads in Addis were so uneven that we used those marble floors as our skate rink, grasping the staircase bannister to save ourselves from falls.

One of my first memories in Ethiopia was a bit of an embarrassing one. On my first day of school I went to find a bathroom. I found what turned out to be a faculty bathroom, and unbeknownst to me this particular bathroom had a faulty door. I locked myself in. I had to yell for help for a good ten to fifteen minutes. I was mortified, as of course the story spread through International Community School. The new girl, a redhead, got locked in the bathroom. Later I cried, I raged that I shouldn't be there anyway. What a way to start this new phase in my life. I was also bullied by some girls towards the beginning of that year, but I only cried in private and eventually they let me be and we became friends.

Eventually I settled in alright. Made new friends, the school felt more free as it was the first school I had ever been to that did not have a uniform. But there was still something wrong inside me. At one point, I was diagnosed with clinical depression. I had some suicidal ideation. I was placed on Paxil. The government wanted to send me to an institutional school back in the US, away from my family. Luckily they took in account a letter I wrote in which I was incensed that they would suggest taking me away from my family. So I got to stay where I was – but I had to see a therapist.

I felt broken.

Luckily I had made some friends; this was where I first met one of my current best friends, Svea. It turned out that when we both left Ethiopia, we also both went to Sweden and were to attend the same school there. From these sets of circumstances, we got to know each other well and became best friends pretty quickly. It has been sixteen years now since I first met Svea, and we have never had a fight. I believe she is the only close friend that has reached such a milestone with me.

While there, my father and I started learning Swedish as we knew that would be our next station. We attended St Lucia events at the Swedish school, and Svea would write notes to me in Swedish so that I could learn. At the time I was not good enough to read them yet. Later, in Sweden, I pulled them out one day. Now I was fully aware of the rude things she had written to me. She's lucky I love her, that's all I have to say about that. Ha ha.

Through the Immanuel Evangelical Church youth group, and through school, I met the Ashbys, Ethan and Cathy. Cathy was a bit older, but we got along well enough, Ethan was in my grade and somehow we became best friends.

Through the first six months, I faithfully wrote letters to and read letters from Wyatt. Many of these letters were sexually explicit, especially the ones coming from him. As for myself, I was uncomfortable writing like that and would only write a line or two when he pushed me for it. Unfortunately, I was embarrassed to find out later, my dad had become suspicious and had read some of those letters from Wyatt. But dad kept his mouth shut for a while, hoping I would work it out myself.

One day I wrote a letter to Wyatt. I wasn't stupid. I had learned not to talk about other boys with him. But I did not see the issue mentioning that "youth group this week was at Cathy and Ethan's house." So much for "youth group," so much for "Cathy" – the word that stood out to him was "Ethan."

What followed was an eleven page return letter, a rant reaming me for that mention of Ethan. If you can call a written word a "shout," then Wyatt was shouting at me through those pages – nay, he was screaming. Apparently I was screwing Ethan. I was a whore. I was a slut. I was a bitch. I was once again reduced to filth and made to feel worthless. I read through every word; the degradation jumping out at me from those pages. A hard copy of the abusive words he had screamed in my face more than enough times before.

31

The last page was an apology. I still remember his "apology" verbatim. He apologized for "having to yell" at me, but I "had to know what [I] did was wrong."

Wait, what *I* did wrong? This struck a chord in me finally. I had been feeling a bit guilty for my compliance in the previous sexual acts, but suddenly it all became clear. What *I* did wrong? How *dare* he?

I decided right then that it had to be over. My family happened to go over to the Ashby's that night. I took the letter with me and had Ethan read it. He and I were outside chatting and I sobbed on his shoulder. I remember handing him that ring Wyatt had given me and asking him to get rid of it. I thanked my lucky stars that night that I was in Ethiopia and that I did not have to see him or be taken advantage by him again. I did not have to fear his retribution.

Over a decade later, I 'ran into' Wyatt again online. I thought "What the hell, we're grownups now" and got into a conversation with him. I was curious as to if he had changed. He told me he was still in love with me. I told him I had a hard time believing that. He didn't even know me, not really. He said he always loved me, he knew if I hadn't have left we would be married with kids by now. The thought scared me. He didn't seem to remember how we broke up. He only remembered that our relationship dissolved because of distance. Even then, with him hundreds of miles away, I was too chicken shit to contradict him. At that time he was barely making ends meet. I thought to myself "I dodged a bullet." I would have been poor with a bunch of kids most likely if I had run off with him like we had planned. I also suspect that the abusive nature of our relationship would have escalated, quite possibly leaving me as a battered wife.

He was messaging me a bit after that, talking about love – overstepping boundaries, I decided. So I ended up cutting him off again. I heard a little later he ended up getting married. I want to be the bigger person; I want to be able to wish him well, but I am ever so glad I moved on from him. I broke free almost two years to the day from our first date. Two years was enough to start shaping my self-esteem and relationship psyche.

৪০৫৪

In Ethiopia, I came across my first real experience with Christian Judgement. The disapproving looks and snotty remarks if you didn't meet "Christian" expectations. More focused than the Fresta Valley feeling of being judged. Bless him, but Ethan was guilty of it with me. So were the rest of his family, as well as other friends from church. I am still friends with Ethan, and I don't blame him or think that he was ever a bad guy. I believe he thought he was doing right in trying to periodically counsel me when I would supposedly stray from my Christian walk. Unfortunately, he was also fifteen, he was not properly equipped to take that role, he wasn't equipped to help a girl who had been damaged like me. I recall hinting to him about some of the sexual things that had happened to me, and in turn he told his mum – who told my mum that I was "*promiscuous.*" That word just drips with judgement.

 He also didn't realize what these kinds of disapproving looks like his parents would give could do to a girl, to anyone, really. This was a seed planted in me that started my distrust of *evangelicals*.

When I say "evangelicals" I refer to the often charismatic evangelical Christians, though the word is also associated with denominations that don't necessarily fit the bill of the type of Christian I am talking about. I will note here that not all evangelicals fit this stereotype, but once I broke from these kinds of people and joined the Lutheran Church, it took me years to go back and make friends and even, as now, attend a women's Bible study at an evangelical church.

৪০৫৪

At the International Community School, I got my first true taste of theatre kid life. I've always been a bit of a ham, and loved doing school plays and nativities as a child, but during those I was always an angel, a sheep, or in one I remember being a hobgoblin with one line. At ICS, I got the first

33

experience with a 'real' role, as well as with an actual theatre class. At ICS, I played Fyedka in *The Fiddler on the Roof.*

I played a male part because there were not enough boys that had auditioned. I was not the only girl playing male parts at least – so I didn't need to feel so self-conscious about it. This was only the beginning for my love affair with the stage. Before leaving Ethiopia, I got a part in a theatre troupe's kids pantomime show. I can't remember what it was, but I ended up having to leave before it got performed as Ethiopia went to war with Eritrea in 1998. All non-essential personnel and families were evacuated. This meant my family left, sans my dad who had to stay to finish his tour there.

Chapter 7

"But, my God, it's so beautiful when the boy smiles."

&Anna Nalick

At the end of 1998, my sisters, mum, and I went to live with my maternal grandparents for a while to avoid the Ethiopia-Eritrea war, and to wait for my dad. I remember in those days my mum was constantly on the computer and reading newspapers with a worried expression on her face.

My grandparents lived in Frederick, MD. Up through to this point in my life I had always considered Frederick as home. It was the base location to which our family returned almost yearly for vacations. My grandmother's home was the most familiar and unchanging place for me – until they sold it a few years later.

Since I was about to turn sixteen, and we knew we would be there for a while, I was enrolled into Frederick High School for the spring of 1999. My time at Frederick High was pretty happy and relatively carefree. The lessons seemed easier, except that I took Advanced English and that had a tough teacher. I remember I took Algebra and Art – but the class that had the most effect on me was my theatre class.

Theatre class is where I made most of my school friends, and where I met Andre and Justin. I don't remember the specifics of how everything started, our first introductions, but I dated Andre, a British boy, for a few weeks while at the same time becoming fast friends with Justin. For some reason, I don't recall why, Andre and Justin did not get along. I remember them fighting nearly every day. I remember telling Andre to cut it out, because Justin was my friend. One day it got physical, so I broke up with Andre. Two weeks later Justin asked me out and I agreed. At sixteen I was oblivious to the implications of what happened, but looking back – boy I come off as a bitch!

Recently, Justin and I reminisced about those times and he had forgotten the fighting. He said he remembered not liking Andre much, but didn't hate him or anything. Brushing it off as being immature sixteen year old boys. When I reminded him of the timeline and why I broke up with Andre, he exclaimed "No wonder Andre hated me!"

36

I've always felt bad for the way I treated Andre then. He was a sweet boy. We did remain friends for a while, and even gave it another go when we were around nineteen. Unfortunately it did not work, and we ceased contact shortly thereafter.

Justin and I dated for about three months. We knew the whole time that I would be leaving by the end of the semester, but we didn't care. We effectively ignored the impending date. I remember my relationship with Justin as just plain fun. I remember staying up half the night- talking on the phone for four or five hours. I remember trips to the mall and the movies. Recently he reminded me of holding hands in theatre class and the teacher, Mr Tempton, breaking us apart and taking him aside to give him a "man-to-man" talk about respecting women. As if holding his girlfriend's hand in class was disrespectful. I remember laughing about that.

Unfortunately the end came up quickly. We discussed trying to do long distance, but in the end he decided he couldn't handle that and called to break up with me. I know it would have never worked. We were too young to make something like that work, and it would have been unfair to restrict ourselves, but at the time I was heartbroken. I was upset he couldn't tell me this to my face. I remember running to my friend, Ashley's, house and crying in her room. I told this to Justin recently too. He said that hearing that made him feel like a schmuck, ha ha. But it was a break up and that's how break ups work.

I am not proud of my behaviour directly after the breakup. I was angry and hurt and said things I shouldn't have said. But luckily we made up and decided to leave on friendly terms. So, even though we go significant periods of time without chatting, we are still friends and keep in touch. Incidentally, we now both have daughters named Emma that were born a month apart. This was unplanned, but I think it's pretty neat.

Theatre class fuelled my passion for being on stage. In the theatre, on the stage, you can be whoever you want to be. You can pretend that you aren't yourself. I learned more about blocking, about improv. I was told by my teacher once that I had great "stage presence" and this made me feel good about myself. I realized I actually had a real talent I could build on.

I got my first try at writing a play, just a one act and along with two other people, but it turned out pretty well I thought. My first try at a monologue. My first experience with a proper theatre stage. It helped that I knew the classes I was doing were merely to pass time and would not affect my eventual graduation credits. I was thoroughly enjoying myself.

ᛞᏨ

Another big aspect of my life in Frederick for those few months was Young Life. By this time in my life I had been fully ingrained into the evangelical youth culture, so it was a natural step to become involved with such a youth organization. I have nothing bad to say about Young Life. I always had a great time, made good friends, and did not feel judged. That was a big deal. This part of it is what kept me a Christian over the years. These were some formative years in which I started to discover what I really believe and formed the part of me that would come back around to Christianity even after later times in which I had started to turn away.

Young Life is an organization that is not overly in your face about Christianity. They had a Bible study weekly for the actual Christian kids, and then right after would be the regular meeting. These meetings were designed for secular kids to come, have fun, and start learning about God in a non-threatening not-in-your-face kind of way. In this atmosphere it made it okay to not be a "perfect Christian."

Chapter 8

"I have come home at last! This is my real country! I belong here. This is the land I have been looking for all my life, though I never knew it till now...Come further up, come further in!"

~C.S. Lewis,
The Last Battle

In the summer of 1999 we moved to Stockholm, Sweden. Up to this point, Australia had been my favourite place I had lived. Sweden very quickly took top billing. I loved Sweden. I fit there. Most of my life people, much to my annoyance, would tell me not to be so quiet, to smile more, to be more outgoing – even when I had literally only just met the person. In Sweden the average person is much more reserved. The average personality was basically my personality. I fit in and it just felt right.

Before we arrived my mum had found out that there was a Young Life group in Stockholm and that they had a camp happening with in a week of our arrival date. She got it all arranged so that I could attend. Boy was I tired, but it was a great way to be introduced to the country. I got to meet a few kids that would be going to my school, friends that would become and remain good friends.

I was also lucky to have Svea already in town. She took me under her wing to show me around, and then when school started she was there as well – though she was in a different class. She was in a Natural Sciences line while I started in International Baccalaureate with Elena and Anneke – two friends from camp. Both Svea and I were held back a year because of our ages as Swedish kids graduate on average a year or two later than American curriculum kids do. At the time I was really irritated about it, but in hindsight I'm glad as it meant one extra year that I could live in Sweden.

During the summer, Svea and I also decided that I needed a new name, to reinvent myself a bit and to start anew at this new school. After much discussion, it was decided she would now call me "Rae."

Young Life was much the same in Sweden as it was in America. It was primarily run by American ex-patriots, so it was based on the same model and just tweaked for their Swedish kid audience. I attended two camps at Holsby Brunn with them while living there, and went to several weekly meetings – though at the time they were only held in Täby which was a suburb on the other side of the city than me, so I didn't always get up and go.

As a family we started going to New Life church. We went primarily because it spoke English. It was actually pretty neat that they would preach in both English and Swedish. Whichever the preacher spoke in, there was a translator for the opposite language. This made services twice as long, but eventually they moved from the old theatre they were occupying to a Finnish school auditorium so they set up tables and people would be able to drink their tea and eat some pastries while the service was going on. This was lovely, and personally helped me to keep attention so I assume that was part of the goal.

I did not have an issue with the church itself, or the leaders of the church, but my time related to that church changed my view of Christianity, especially evangelical Christianity, forever. The start of it was that I went to several youth group events, attended most Sundays, and then wouldn't be there for a month. I would come back and some main youth kids wouldn't even remember who I was. They'd be friendly enough, but they would be reintroducing themselves to me. I remember telling one of the pastor's sons that we've met before, because I've been there several times. He said "Oh, yes! You do look familiar. You are Dutch, right?" No. No I am not. That would be Anneke.

I felt invisible.

If you can't even remember my face, how can I matter to you?

I would think that if I had a boyfriend, it should be a good Christian boy. But any boy that I met in the church would turn me down saying I wasn't their "type." Even a few times when I wasn't even looking for a date, just trying to be friendly. What the hell was wrong with me that I wasn't the right "type" for a "good, Christian, boy?" This weighed on my self-esteem for quite a long while. I know it's silly, but I wondered if they could somehow tell that I wasn't so pure anymore.

The big event that happened that drew me away was something else entirely. I had become good friends with three sisters. By the time this all happened I was a senior in Gymnasium. I was about eighteen and nineteen years old, and the oldest sister had moved to the US to start University. The spring of my senior year I moved in with the family to finish off the school year as my dad had retired mid-year and had to go back to the States.

The middle sister had had a falling out with her parents at this time. They were staunch Christians and they did not approve that she had slept with her boyfriend, so they kicked her out. They didn't want her influence on the youngest. Lucky they didn't know I had lost my virginity by then as well. They would argue in the kitchen, while I sat in my room. "Well if Rae acted like that, we wouldn't let you hang out with her either!" I closed my eyes and thought "Please don't drag me into this."

It was really uncomfortable in that house when there would be fighting. The youngest just wanted to be able to see her sister. They would try to accept her back a bit and gain her trust by inviting her over for dinner and then start fighting with her again.

The pastors of the church even counselled the parents that they should love and accept their daughter. That kids will make mistakes, but parents should love and accept, pray and be patient. These parents would have none of it.

This family had been very active in the church for many years, and this middle sister had had many good friends amongst the youth. At least she thought she had good friends. She told me that from the "church" kids I was the only one left that would speak to her, along with one other girl that had left the church a while back. They effectively cut her off. Where was the love and acceptance? It's no wonder that she was driven away from Christianity. It took her years to come back to God, years and years.

ೲ

42

This family also tried to impose a curfew on me. 10 PM for a nineteen year old? Were they kidding? Not only was I over eighteen, but my own parents hadn't given me any such curfew even before my eighteenth birthday. I was a teenager in Stockholm, Sweden. It would be nearly unheard of even for a younger teen to be put on a 10 PM curfew. I was used to 2 AM home times by this age. Because of this, and the uncomfortable atmosphere that often hung in the house, I spent almost every weekend at Svea's apartment.

Around this time, Svea's mum, step-dad, and little sister would spend almost every weekend at their summer or their winter houses out of town. This meant Svea and I could play house. We would go buy groceries, rent some movies, and cook fancy meals for ourselves before settling down to watch our movies. Occasionally going out to the bars with our friends or to parties at night, but that was not an every weekend event.

Svea's mum and step-dad, Anna and Anders, always made me feel welcome in their home. As a side note: in Sweden kids call their parents, friend's parents, and teachers by their first names. My dad felt so Swedish when Svea would call him "Karl." He was not-so-secretly pleased by this.

I remember going to Svea's winter house in Borka for 2002 winter sport break. There are two weeks a year that kids get out of school for time to do sport. One in the autumn and one in the winter. This year we had a bunch of homework, so we went to her house with her family. On their property they had an old, no central heating, guest house. It was our house. We stoked the pot belly stove, we sat in the kitchen to do homework and drink tea. It was a lovely time. We walked her chocolate lab, Frankie-boy, through the snow covered woods. We laughed as Frankie chased "bears." Really he was just thinking he was tough growling at small animals or clusters of trees.

We cross country skied across the frozen lake. I could actually do cross country skiing without falling down (as opposed to regular downhill skiing.) That is, until I tried to go over a small incline.

We long distance skated on the lake as well. After all this, and after putting my boot through the ice into frigid water, we made our way into the big, main house that had heated floors and the sauna.

ೞೞ

I remember trips to Svea's summer house in Sandhamn as well. What I wouldn't give to go there with her again. We always went alone when we did, her family usually doing something else. This house was a small old cabin that her grandparents had built. It was a small living room area with a small bedroom off the side and a later addition of a kitchen connected. It had another small building to the side that held more beds. In between both buildings was a small bathroom building with an eco-toilet.

To get to Sandhamn we had to take a train to catch a bus that took forty-five minutes or so to reach the harbour. Then we would hop a ferry that would go to various islands off the coast of Stockholm. Sandhamn often has yachts all around it as it is one of the main harbours for the yearly yacht race held out that way. One side of the island is a little more tourist oriented with a hotel, a couple restaurants, and the small grocery store. We would get off at the next dock on the other side. Sandhamn had beautiful ocean views, and then you'd turn around and see forest of green. Tall, green trees covering most of the island. We would have to go to the grocery store sometimes, or go get an ice cream, so we would walk through these serene woods for about ten minutes until we reached the other side of the island.

When I think of my happy place, I imagine myself lying out on the deck of Svea's summer house in Sandhamn... Svea by my side as we smoke, eat tomatoes and salt, and drink a cider or two.

<u>Chapter 9</u>

"Acting is behaving truthfully under imaginary circumstances."

୨୦*Sanford Meisner*

The school I attended in Sweden was Kungsholmens Gymnasium on the suburb island of Kunsgholmen. It was a ways away from my home on Lidingö, especially since public transportation was the main way to get around town; there are no separate school busses in Stockholm. I walked ten minutes to the bus stop, caught a train at Ropsten, switched to another train at T-Centralen, and then walked another ten minutes after getting off at Fridhemsplan. All-in-all my average trip was about forty-five minutes. Luckily the system was very good, safe, and clean. Even at night. It also was a freeing experience to be able to go anywhere I wanted whenever I wanted.

My school was a beautiful old building that had seven floors, and no elevator. Well, they did have an elevator for teachers and disabled students to use, but it required a key and alas I was without one when I would be on the bottom floor with a class in two minutes on the sixth.

I really enjoyed my time at Kungsholmens. It had open-campus and the teachers treated us as though we were adults. This resulted in students that were much more mature than you would expect from many American High Schools. I started 10th grade in the International Baccalaureate line, but soon decided that I would rather do Social Sciences, partially because I could do theatre class in that line and IB kids had no such option. I had to be put on a waiting list, but made it into the ESb class by the beginning of the second semester.

In ESb I met another life-long friend. Actually I guess you could say several because there are a few that I am still in touch with, but Maja was and still is classified amongst my best friends. Maja was a Canadian-Iranian girl that had moved to Sweden to live with her strict (and a bit crazy, I'd suspect) aunt after her parents had died.

Maja and I went just about everywhere together, especially at school. We were in the same class, so we had almost all the same classes to attend as it was, but we were also rarely apart in between classes. Usually if we were not together it was because I was with Dan and she only barely tolerated him for my sake.

ೞ‌ೞ

I took my theatre pretty seriously then. I became co-chair of the drama club along with my friend, Linus. One main memory I have from that club was an improv game we once played. It was called "Freeze!" or something like that and in this game there would be two people doing an improv scene and someone in the audience would shout "Freeze!" before coming up, taking one of the positions and starting off a new scene.

Linus and I started the game this day. Linus started it off in a direction of violence and a girlfriend beating scene. He never laid a hand on me, but we fed off of each other and I effectively reacted with tears, and shaking, and apparently it looked very much like he was striking me and throwing me around. The rest of the club was shocked, watching, not sure of what to do. Eventually another boy yelled "Freeze!" as he jumped up from his chair. Linus's foot froze mid-kick, an inch from my head. The boy then took over the scene without a clue of what to do and the game fell apart from there. I was told after the fact that they all really thought he was hurting me, and after the assurance that I was not hurt they were then impressed with our skill. I was now one of those theatre kids; it had become ingrained in my personality.

I continued on with theatre class, and doing theatre competitions. Every year the Year 2 classes would compete in a Shakespeare day and the Year 3 classes would compete in a Drama day. Both years my class won – well, we tied with our sister class ESa for Shakespeare day.

For Shakespeare day our class decided to a death and dying compilation instead of just one play. We did Julius Caesar, Romeo and Juliet... Not sure on what else, but also Othello. Othello was our finale as there are a good four or five deaths all around the end of the play. I was in Othello as the main part of Desdemona.

Nikolai played Iago, and Jude was Othello. I remember being so irritated with Jude because he had only shown up for one rehearsal. I was dreading the show because I was so sure he'd end up fucking it up because I thought he didn't care. At the last rehearsal he was not there again, so I called and screamed at him over the phone.

I did not see him again until right before the show. He showed up with a shaved head and a sharpie tattoo drawn on his head to match the Othello from the movie. He blew it out of the park. I don't know if he was actually just that good at remembering lines, or if he had realized he was going to let me down if he didn't buckle down and do it right.

While on stage, as the story goes, Othello smothers Desdemona... and as the story doesn't say – Desdemona kicked Othello in the face. I didn't realize I had even done that until I was told by Maja afterwards. Luckily Jude thought it was and still is hilarious. He actually apologized to me (with tongue in cheek) for his "iron jaw."

For Drama day the next year, our class decided to do Woody Allen's *Bullets Over Broadway.* I condensed and wrote the script to fit the allotted time, was an assistant director, and played the part of Helen Sinclair. Maja played my Manager.

I had decided in Gymnasium that I wanted to be an actress, or at the very least a theatre teacher. By senior year I had a gruff Welsh theatre teacher. He was relatively young, but disfigured by a large scar across his face. When senior examinations came around, I had to perform a Bedbound monologue, an Antigone monologue and a Moliere dialogue with a partner. We went in to the room in pairs to be examined. Luckily we went first. My heart was pounding in my chest. I eased my tension by making a joke. He laughed – that was a good sign. My partner and I turned out to be the only ones in the class to make a perfect grade. Most others barely passed, if at all. Apparently our gruff Welsh teacher was put into a bad mood rather quickly. I felt exhilarated when it was all over. But then I started to wonder if I wanted to live my whole life with knots in my stomach and my heart pounding in my ears as I climb on stage to be watched and judged again and again. Was the after effect of exhilaration really worth it?

Chapter 10

"We return to the lives of those who have gone before us,
a perplexing mobius strip, until we come home,
eventually, to ourselves."

&Colum McCann,
TransAtlantic

Living in Sweden felt like home. I think this, coupled with the particular age I was at the time, is why I have so much to say about events that happened there. There is a whole other reason that Sweden was like home: my family heritage traces back to there. My grandfather on my mother's side remembers his father and grandparents still speaking Swedish, especially when they would receive letters from the motherland. My grandmother on that side is of German lineage. My father's side also has a large Swedish base, coupled with a large amount of Dutch.

My mother dedicated herself to researching our family history in Sweden. We made several trips around to different research centres, libraries, and churches. At some point she discovered that Oskar Englund was a man that lived at Axmarsbruk. He had had ten children, half of whom travelled to the USA in the early 1900s. One of which, Helga, had married another Swedish emigrant with the name of Bernhard Ericson. These were my grandfather's grandparents.

Armed with this information, my mum planned a trip. We went to Axmarsbruk to take a little look around. Now all that is there is the *bruk,* or factory, where they used to make iron. There are also a few summer cabins scattered in the woods and an old warehouse-turned-restaurant by the water. My great-great-great-grandfather's house had burned down a long time ago, but we could locate where it had stood.

In those days, my dad had a tradition of taking us each out for dinner and a movie of our choice for our birthdays. When my eighteenth birthday came around, he asked me where I wanted to go. Joking, I said "The restaurant at Axmarsbruk." It was a two hour drive away, so I really didn't expect it when he answered "Alright." It may be silly to drive two hours just for dinner, but that restaurant was *really* good.

We walked through the wood picking up the greenish blue rocks that were by-products of the iron factory having functioned there long ago. We found Oskar's photo in the little museum above the restaurant. We came across some people on the road and my mum asked some questions about the area and mentioned we were researching the Englund family. The lady said that someone she knew was from the Englund family of this area. Through this chance meeting we got to meet all of our living relatives. There was one still living near the area, but others we travelled around Sweden to meet. We met one old female relative who walked to the shore in Axmarsbruk and told us of dances they used to hold out here, and how she got into mischief – riding off on the handlebars of a handsome boy's bicycle. She also remembered the family growing potatoes across the lake, and told of how her sister and she had to go by boat to tend and harvest them. Even then I enjoyed listening to old people reminisce.

We went to Gävle and Vingåker. We looked through old records at Hemrånge Kyrka before going to have lunch with my great aunt. Hemrånge Kyrka is a strange pink colour on the outside, but otherwise it is a beautiful old Lutheran church, all of our Axmarsbruk family records were contained there. I thought that maybe one day it would be nice to get married there. The heritage aspect appealed to me, and the small church that Oskar had preached at in Axmarsby was now a museum and wouldn't do.

I looked at all the confirmation pictures on the wall in the office, noticing one particular attractive boy. When we got to my great aunt's house I saw this same boy's picture on the mantel. Turns out he was my second cousin.

My mum always took me or my sister Sarah with her because we were better at Swedish than her and English was not required in schools until the 1970s, so many of the older relatives couldn't speak it well, if at all. We were so embarrassed when she would try to speak Swedish. Not because of her accent or not pronouncing something right, but because she didn't really know more than a few words so she would try to compensate by speaking loudly and saying English words but trying to make them sound Swedish. Oh Lord. I would just have to shake my head and walk away to hide my embarrassment sometimes. Later, after we moved back to the States, I was also the one required to read postcards and letters they had sent to my mum.

Because of this sudden rush of success finding family, my mum arranged a family reunion at a park near Axmarsbruk. My grandparents flew in for it, as did my grandfather's cousin, Olle Englund. Olle had married a Swedish woman, Inga, and though they lived in California, they made yearly trips to Sweden anyway.

I attended the reunion, but went off on my own when a group of the relatives took a tour around the bruk that had been arranged. I wish now I hadn't missed it. I wish I had gotten the most I could out of these experiences.

<u>Chapter 11</u>

*"Of all sad words of tongue or pen, the saddest are these,
'it might have been.'"*

*~John Greenleaf Whittier,
Maud Muller - Pamphlet*

I used to pride myself in my attention to detail. I am usually quite observant and I always thought I had a talent for figuring people out. I think maybe I do have a slight talent for it, but I have also realized that I can be pretty oblivious to what is really going on around me sometimes. Maybe certain people are just better at hiding cues for me to notice.

I have discovered a few times, after it is too late to do anything about, that a certain guy had a crush on me or something. One that really stands out in my mind was a guy named Thomas that I went to school with in Ethiopia. He was also an American, in the same class, and we both were getting therapy.

One year for Valentine's Day our school had a fete and all the classes put together something to sell for fundraising around the school. Our class decided to make a book of love poems that various students submitted work for. When it came out, I flipped through it. Thomas had submitted two poems and they by and large stood out above all the others. They were very well written. Both of them were about unrequited love. One, written in first person, was about committing suicide after not being able to have the girl he was in love with. I still remember the last line: "The last thing I heard was a comforting click." The click in question being from a gun held to [his] head.

I remember reading this and being concerned for his mental health. I asked him if he was alright. He replied that he was fine, it was just fiction.

At the end of that term Thomas moved to India. Incidentally, he went to India and attended school with and became friends with Linus – the guy that co-chaired the drama club in Sweden with me. What a small world.... But I digress. After he left, my mother mentioned to me that it was too bad I never got together with Thomas. I was unsure of why she said that, so I questioned her. Well, it turns out that she was friends with his mother. They had chatted, as friends do, and his mum told mine that those two poems he had written were about me.

I had never thought about him that way, but I can honestly say I would have given him a chance if he had let me know. Oh well and *c'est la vie*. The past has passed.

୫୦୯

Speaking of being oblivious: in Sweden, there was a classmate of ours named Jude, as mentioned. I thought he was cool, and I liked him, but we didn't really hang out all that much outside of class. Maja hung out with him a little more, but not by much. He was a bit of a thug back then – but I hadn't even realized how much until years later when another classmate told me things he used to do to her and her friends. This included stealing and harassing. I'm glad to say he is a changed man now and eventually contacted her to apologize and make amends for his youthful indiscretions.

At the time I was oblivious to all that. I don't know how I could have been, but I was. The real shocker to me, however; was that one day in late Year 2 or early Year 3, he came up to Maja and me out in the courtyard. He told us that he wanted us to know that he cared for us, that we were his girls (in a 'homie' kind of way), and that if any guy ever hurt us to let him know and he would deal with them. When he walked away with that swagger of his, I turned to Maja and said "I didn't realize Jude and I were such good friends."

Jude is a ranger and a wildlife photographer in South Africa now. He goes by his initials because he doesn't want to associate himself with his old life by using his first name like he did back then. I've kept up with him, but it has mostly been generic how-do-you-dos and just checking in on his beautiful pictures once in a while. Then, in 2010 he surprised me again. He sent me a message out of the blue. He seemed down and he wanted advice. We had a lovely conversation and I hope that he was telling the truth when he said I helped and that I made him smile. Once again I was surprised. I was surprised that I was who he thought of to go to.

In 2005, after Hurricane Katrina, I had moved to Tennessee. There I received a card in the mail. It was from an old classmate from ESb as well. His name was Jack and he had heard about what happened to us in the Hurricane. I don't remember even talking all that much with Jack at school, so it was a fair surprise to receive that too. In the card he told me that he thought it was great that I had picked myself up, dusted myself off and was getting on with life. He told me he was proud of me. All of this made me wonder how many people I have ignored friendships from. Not on purpose, but just because I was oblivious to the signs that they wanted to be or saw themselves as my friend. I just hope I am doing a better job at it now, but I suspect that I still fail in this area.

ଚଠଗ

As this chapter seems to have a theme of missed chances, I will now tell you about Martijn. I met Martijn when I first moved to Sweden at the Young Life camp. He was Anneke's older brother; he was handsome, smart, and kind. I had a major crush on him.

We went on one date that summer. I believe it was to see *The Matrix* at the Cinema. It was a nice time, but soon after school started. We went to the same school, but our schedules differed enough that I rarely saw him. I did, however; go fairly often to his house when I would have sleepovers with Anneke. He wasn't always there, but when he was I was focused on activities with Anneke.

Anneke told me once that nearly every friend of hers had a crush on Martijn. She said that she approved of me dating him because I was the only friend with a crush that had come over for a sleepover and would not abandon her in order to flirt with her brother all night.

Martijn was a good, Christian guy. I didn't think he liked me that way. All the other good, Christian guys didn't like me that way after all. We did have a couple nice chats over those first two years, but then he graduated and moved back to Holland to go to University.

The next year, he came back for a visit the week Anneke was to get baptised. I knew he was there, but didn't think to call him or anything as we had never gotten too close. Anneke wanted me at her Baptism since I was one of her best friends, so I obliged. I saw Martijn across the crowded church, nodded a hello, and then the service started.

Afterwards, everyone was crowding around the newly baptised members and it was a bit chaotic so I decided to leave and just call her up a little later. I pushed my way out of the church and started up the road. Within seconds, Martijn had come running out of the church frantically calling my name. I know, right? Starting to sound like a cheesy novel, ha ha! But that is what happened. I stopped and turned. He caught up with me. He said he was so glad he hadn't missed me while he was back. He asked me to go out with him the next day. Surprised, and honestly pleased, I agreed and we made arrangements. Then he turned and walked back into the church.

The next day was one of the loveliest dates I have ever been on, if I'm honest. We walked all around town together; it was a beautiful fair weather day. We went to a café; we stopped by a pier on Djursholm to have a beer overlooking the water. We literally spent the entire day together. It was an eight hour date.

At the café, Martijn told me that he was starting to consider marriage. He wanted to get married and start a family shortly after University. He said he felt like that is what is supposed to happen. He told me he wasn't sure if he'd find a woman while in University that he'd want to marry. He asked me to make a pact with him. He said "If neither of us finds someone before the end of University, will you marry me?"

I didn't even have to think. I said yes.

Only a year and a half later I was back in the US. I was getting proposed to. I emailed Martijn the next day to tell him what happened. I'm not sure if Martijn ever really thought that it would happen between us, but he emailed me back "So much for our plans, ha ha." He congratulated me.

At one point my mum found out about this story. I had thought she knew, but apparently I never mentioned it before. At the time she was mad at my husband and she exclaimed "Why did you marry Jason when you could have had Martijn?!" Well, mum, I couldn't *not* live my life on the off chance that Martijn wouldn't find someone else to love. He was a very attractive man, after all.

Around that time, my mum was constantly trying to convince me that my marriage was a mistake, since she and my husband were not getting along. She did not stop until I finally told her I would never speak to her again if she said even one more disparaging remark about him.

Luckily Martijn found a woman that he married within a couple years, a while after he graduated. I have lost touch directly with him now, but Anneke tells me he is doing well and last I heard he is a diplomat in Serbia.

Chapter 12

"No apologies. He'll never see you cry. Pretends he doesn't know that he's the reason why you're drowning."

∞Taylor Swift,
I Knew You Were Trouble

Since I was a teenager in Sweden, an older teenager, naturally many of my relationships happened there. Dan – Danny – was my main attraction during Gymnasium. But Viktor was my first actual boyfriend while there. There is not a whole lot to say about this largely unremarkable relationship. Except that I lost my virginity to him. I debate over whether to consider myself a virgin at that point because of what went on with Wyatt, but Viktor was the first boy I had intercourse with. I still remember the date – December 6th, 1999.

The only reasoning I have for doing it with him is that we were both virgins and we wanted to get over the awkwardness of a first time. Who better to do it with than someone you don't love? It was painful the first time for me, and I was glad that I didn't have to be embarrassed by any of that for someone I really liked later.

I know as an upstanding Lutheran woman I should look back at my premarital sex and say I am ashamed of my past. But I'm not, so I'm not going to lie. It may not have been the best choice, may not have been the best man to do it with even, but it was far from the worst. As Rizzo would say, "There are worse things I could do."

Viktor and I dated for three months. We got along okay and he was nice enough. But his sense of humour irked me and we just didn't fit. I was afraid of hurting his feelings, but eventually I gathered up the courage and broke up with him. He told me the next day that he was a bit sad at first, but by the time he was on the train home he felt a large weight lift off of him and had realized he felt much the same I had in our relationship.

಴ಂಐ

Now. Now it's time to talk about Danny. His real name is Daniel, most people called him Dan. I preferred him as Danny. I liked Danny from the moment I saw him. He was a British Swede. More British in look and attitudes, he had lived a fair amount of his childhood in Britain after all, but his mother was fully Swedish. Though I never met his parents, his father was a jovial Brit, and always seemed pleased when I would call their house for Dan.

My friends thought I was crazy, though Svea at one point admitted that she could see why I was attracted to him. Dan and I were never exclusively together, but we had a thing. This thing lasted on and off for the whole three years I was there. I am still not sure how to classify our thing, our tumultuous thing.

Dan was two years older than I, though he was only one grade above me. Not because he wasn't smart, in fact I'm pretty sure he was a genius. The year before I met him, however; he just rarely turned up for school and hadn't done any of the work so he was kept behind. When I met him he had pulled his act together in that regard and was actually attending and trying to graduate.

Dan usually came to school in scruffy clothes and a trench coat. He would sit in the courtyard smoking cigarettes with his friends. As I would find as I got to know him, he also did drugs with these friends. He was stoned much of the time, and from what I gathered was often on amphetamines. He was a dark figure and, as they say, girls are attracted to bad boys. Dan was my bad boy.

From what I remember, I saw this dark boy. This brown eyed boy, and was immediately attracted to him. I made myself be bold. I went up and introduced myself. I introduced myself as "Rae," because I was starting my new image.

It started slowly, but from the beginning he would acknowledge me in the halls. Eventually we started going out some. If I remember correctly our first date was to see *American Psycho* at the cinema in Hötorget. I was surprised to see him waiting for me in a nice sweater, and his shoes were not scuffed. I commented on how nice he looked. He told me there was nothing else clean.

He would comment through the movie at the skill of the psycho, "Nice aim!" he said as Patrick Bateman dropped the chainsaw from the stairwell and hit his victim. But when he was about to feed a kitten to the ATM, Dan exclaimed "Not the kitty!" Dan made me smile.

Dan and I had fun when we went out, but he did not want to commit to a relationship. He had been scarred by his previous girlfriend. He broke up with her, she threatened suicide. He never saw her again, so he had assumed the worst. He felt guilty. I learned from a mutual friend that the girl had slept with Dan's best friend then left town after the break up and moved in with an older man. He needed to know, but I didn't feel it was my place to say anything.

Another nice memory I have of Dan was one day we decided to meet up and go to a café. We hadn't given consideration to the fact that it was a Sunday and no cafés would be open. So we walked and walked through town, talking and eventually ending up finding a McDonalds. While there he laid his head in my lap, and while we were talking he suddenly put his hand behind my head and brought me forward to kiss him.

I remember lying together on the shore of Lidingö, kissing. I remember skipping classes because we were curled up together in the study room, usually with his head in my lap. How sweet it all seemed at the time.

But life with Dan was not all sunshine and roses. He was my bad boy after all. Dan and I fought a lot. It was a strange relationship in which I did not care when we fought. By that I mean, any other friend or boyfriend I would ever fight with, I would be concerned about making up and right wrongs as soon as possible. But I would walk away from Dan and we wouldn't speak for a week. After this cooling off time we would be back to the way we were as if nothing had ever happened. I don't know that this was a healthy way to handle it, but it was what it was and it seemed to work for us.

He would purposely try to make me mad, to get under my skin. I am not sure why he did such things. Was he testing me? Was he trying to drive me away? One instance I remember was during my Year 2, his senior year. I'm relatively certain we had recently had a disagreement. I walk out into the court yard. Next to him sat this little nothing Year 1 girl that obviously crushed on him that whole year. She hung around like an annoying little gnat. I still remember her name. Kaitlyn. Ugh. I do not know if he chose her because she was just there or because he knew she annoyed me, but when he saw me walk out he grabbed her by the waist and hoisted her onto his lap and started making out with her. Her silly self was obviously pleased – but what she couldn't see is that he was staring at me the entire time. Not creepy at all, Dan.

I didn't give him the time of day that day.

Shortly before he graduated we had a huge fight. At least it was huge to me. We actually talked about considering getting together for real. He was concerned that I was a serious girl that needed a serious relationship. We were too different, my being Christian bothered him. I can attest that I didn't care about all that. I already knew that Dan and I would never last the long run, I just knew I liked and cared for him. He apparently didn't believe that. A few days, maybe even weeks, later he told me to leave and that he didn't even want to be friends anymore. I didn't understand why there was suddenly no friendship even allowed between us. I was so angry with him. The usual silent week turned into several silent months.

He graduated. I didn't call him. The next year was my senior year. I was dating a twenty-five year old Danish man named Sven for a while. Keeping my mind off Dan. Sven proposed. I turned him down. I had a one night stand with a guy named Timmy. I contracted Chlamydia. I kept my mind off of Dan.

One day in early 2002, I looked out a 6th floor window into the courtyard, and I'll be god damned if I didn't see Dan down there. I avoided the courtyard that day. For crying out loud, I had to avoid the courtyard for *days*. I'd see him come down the hall and I would turn the other way. Finally, this tricky bastard showed up in my history class. He sat down right next to me without saying a word. He watched me for an hour. I felt his eyes on me. I ignored him as I fidgeted and nervously shook my foot.

As soon as class was over, I jumped up and left the room without a glance back. What made me think he'd take the hint?

I sat down to have lunch. For some reason Maja, my best friend and boy-buffer, was not around that day. She wasn't there in History; she wasn't there as he sat down across from me in the cafeteria as I ate. I gave up. "Hi, Dan."

 "Hi, Rae."

৪৩৫২

I found out from Maja many years later that she knew why he had so abruptly tried to cut off a relationship with me. That day that we fought about not being friends, I went to the bathroom and sobbed. I wasn't about to let that bastard know he had affected me that way. Maja, in her station as Best Friend Forever, marched her ass out to the courtyard to deal with him. She was ready to have it out with him. She confronted him, luckily omitting the fact I cried over him – I had a rep to protect after all. Apparently during this conversation he admitted that he really cared for me, but he knew that he was "no good" for me and that he wanted me to do better. He liked me, but he didn't want to fuck up my life as he had his own. Maja was defeated as she thoroughly agreed with him. She didn't tell me for years that she had even gone out there, let alone what he had said.

Danny and I saw each other a few more times before I graduated and moved back to the US. No more fighting, though he chickened out at the last minute for our last planned meeting. Saying good bye can be hard, I knew that all too well. So I wasn't angry with him. At least in this time I think I was able to get him to realize that there were people that really cared about him, such as myself. I'm not sure that he had really believed that before. One thing that used to make me angry was comments he would make about things like smoking unfiltered cigarettes so he could die faster. He would say he didn't want to commit suicide because that was the coward's way out, so he'd settle for unfiltered cigarettes. He did not realize the effect those words had on people that cared for him.

Though we fell out of touch for a while, I am glad to say that we are still friends. He is doing well for himself; he is married to what seems to be a lovely lady. He is doing great things. He may not realize this, but I am proud of him.

Chapter 13

"Well, Sinead O'Rebellion, shock me shock me shock me with that deviant behaviour!"

&Gina,
Empire Records

I started going out to bars with friends while I lived in Ethiopia. I was about fifteen, and I would do sleep overs at my friends' houses and we would go out on the town without my parents' knowledge. They did not want me going off around Addis Ababa without trusted companions, and they certainly did not want me to get into any taxis around town. I understand their fears now, but I felt like I needed to be free at that age as well. I never got up to anything too terrible. I was on Paxil then, so I was too afraid to actually drink alcohol knowing that it was a no-no to mix alcohol with my meds. But I still went to bars and dancing with friends. I also recall going with my German friend to the local pool, riding in a taxi. Putting ourselves in a taxi meant we were putting ourselves in a precarious situation as many of them would smoke hashish before getting behind the wheel. Besides the lax traffic laws and lack of traffic lights. After the pool we'd go to her house at the German Embassy compound.

I'm glad my parents did not find out about such antics at the time. This was the one place that had the most security measures that affected my personal life that I remember. We had radios in the house that linked to the Embassy with each family member having registered handles. Ours were based off of Narnia characters. I don't recall what mine or my sisters' were, but my parents were "Aslan" and "Reepicheep." One of them would have to answer back twice a day when the Marines would do a roll call to check on everybody.

I remember one night I was up in my room. My room was a separate apartment on the roof of the house. I had a large living area and a bathroom with a shower. I did not have a kitchen, however; so I still had to come out once in a while. There was a spiral stairwell that went up the side of the house, stopping midway allowing access to the second floor. This night apparently there was an attempted robbery in the house behind us. My dad heard a woman scream and then gunshots. I was oblivious, and fast asleep, until he ran up the stairs banging on my door in his underwear. He had feared it was me. Turned out there was this attempted robbery, and many guards from around the area looked over fences to give their aid and one of them shot at the perp.

৪০৫৩

To get back on topic, I started going to bars when I was fifteen. Once in Sweden, I had more freedom and my parents settled into the Swedish culture well enough. I remember at sixteen I went to a classmate's party where there was some drinking. Not so serious on my part, but I recall my friend Lena leaving with her boyfriend. He had come to pick her up. He was angry for some reason. He was drunk. She got in the car with him. We heard a bang, we smelled burning plastic and the lights went out. We took a look around outside but didn't see anything initially so we went back inside. A little later I was due to be picked up by Elena's mum, so we walked out and got in the car. Then we passed a wreck. It's was Lena's boyfriend's car. They had hit a power box. We jumped out of the car; the police interviewed us a bit. All we knew about Christoff was his name, and that he was twenty. After the police were done asking us questions, I ran back up to the house. I burst through the door screaming for Anneke. Lena was a good friend to us both. I remember Jude racing out the door as soon as he heard what I said. Luckily Lena had injuries that she could recover from, but she was pretty beat up. She hadn't been wearing a seatbelt and had gone through the window. Thank God they weren't going very fast. She was out of school for a while for recovery, however.

In Sweden it was perfectly okay to drink at sixteen as long as parents approved, but you couldn't go to bars until you were eighteen. So until my eighteenth birthday, I did most of my partying at classmate's houses. Once I turned eighteen, however; I started going to bars again. The one most frequented was Monkey Bar. This establishment was around the corner from my school. Maja and I have birthdays that are six days apart, so when we both turned eighteen we went to Monkey Bar together. That first night was on Maja's birthday since hers was after mine.

We started out at Maja's house for a family filled party, her aunt making martinis for us. Then we went on downtown to the bar. What I remember from that night was dancing in the back of the establishment, away from the bar. I started dancing with some guy. He looked me up and down, then said *"Du är fina."* (You are pretty.) "Va?!" I said — I couldn't hear what he said over the music. He leaned in close and said it again. "Tack så mycket," I thanked him. That was all fine and good until I felt like he was backing me up towards the back wall. I called out Maja's name a couple of times until she heard me. She saw the look of panic on my face, so she broke away from the guy she was dancing with and came up and kissed me, calling me *älskling* (darling), thinking that if the guy thought we were lesbians or something he'd think less of the prospect. He backed away saying something about he sees how it is. Maja started dancing with her guy again, this time 'my' guy came back with a friend, they backed me into a dark corner. I screamed and Maja came to my rescue. This time, she looked at her watch and said "OMG! Mum is gonna kill me!! We're late!" She grabbed my hand and yanked me out of the situation and back up to the bar area. Lesson affirmed. Never go out without a trusted friend.

 𝕭𝕺𝕽

Monkey Bar is also where we met two guys — Patrik and Fredrik. I was really attracted to Patrik, but he was dating some girl. I highly jealous girl that would text me awful things when she found out he had met me. Patrik and I never had a relationship. He was not cheating on her at all, but this girl was insecure and came off as a bit nuts. Fredrik and Maja did date a bit after that.

Maja insists that I tell the world what a bitch I am — or was — at this point in my story. She seems to recall that I was annoyed because I had been chatting with those guys first and when she strolled up, her gorgeous Persian self stole the attention. I don't remember all that, but I will admit the plausibility of her memory. I know I had some insecurity being best friends with such a hottie, and it would explain my motivation for my later actions. Anyway, after that night she and Fredrik texted and talked a lot, but it took a while before they were able to organize another meet up. They were supposed to meet at the McDonalds near our school and Maja asked me to come along because when she met him she had been

70

drinking and wasn't positive she remembered correctly what he looked like. When we arrived she reintroduced us saying something about she brought me for safety reasons, since it was a first meet up or something to that effect.

"Actually, she brought me because she couldn't remember what you looked like."

"What the hell, Rae?!"

"Well, I ain't lying."

She was livid.

When Maja reminded me of this story I laughed and said "I'm so glad you are still friends with me, Maja!"

"I didn't want to be friends with you that day!" she exclaimed.

ༀༀ

I remember going to Monkey Bar with Linus and Svea and a few other mutual friends. I recall once going there with them and when I walked in there was a guy at the door that said "Hej!" to me as I walked in. I gave him a frown and said "Hej" back, not impressed with him talking to me. I went and sat down, and ordered my White Russian. A moment later I turned as Svea commented on the fourteen year olds trying to get in, but being stopped at the door. Turned out that guy was the bouncer. I was a little mortified, but I guess I was confident enough that I was allowed to be there that he didn't feel it was necessary to put more effort into checking my ID.

I went to several parties over the years there, mostly with drinking. It wasn't until I was almost eighteen that I discovered my limit – the limit to which I could drink before throwing up. Believe it or not, my limit was pretty high. I only remember snippets of most parties. Not because I didn't remember them at the time, just that they weren't so memorable to last me til my thirties. One thing I do remember was a many parties I would feel like the odd duck out, especially at parties where I only knew one or two people. Guys always seemed to like every other girl at the party except for me. I never understood why, exactly, but it was not great for my self-esteem overall. Jude, a typical popular type boy, remembers me as being "no bombshell" and that with my affinity for wearing vintage and artsy clothing, I did not match up with the girls that typical guys were attracted to. The conversation in which he told me this seems to justify the feelings I had back then. He also told me that he felt that I must have been bullied and let down by men a lot. I hadn't realized that Jude was so observant, especially since we didn't hang out much. But if he noticed these kinds of things about me, I also wonder if I let off some sort of vibe that also affected the way other guys saw me.

While my parents were around, I refrained from having parties at my house. When I moved in with the family friends my last year, however; I do recall throwing one party when they went out of town one weekend. Svea and Linus were there, I don't remember much else about who attended but it was not a huge gathering. All the people that were there were friends from school. The youngest sister was there for a short while. I am not ashamed to say I gave her a drink. Her oldest sister had gone nuts with the alcohol as soon as she was eighteen, and I felt that if the youngest sister felt as repressed the same would happen to her. Then she went off with the middle sister, taking the chance to hang out together while they could and their parents were out of town.

I remember that night arguing with Linus. He got agitated when I would speak to him in English, so he yelled at me in Swedish about how we lived in Sweden, I should address him in Swedish. I laughed and answered him back in English, just to make him mad.

Also, once I turned eighteen, I would start going to Marine parties. I went with Anneke once and Dan once at least. I remember going to one that had a luau theme with a guard from the Embassy named Calle. He was a cutie pie. He was from Kiruna, in the north of Sweden. I also went to a few other parties with him and remember once his sister was visiting and a bunch of us were staying in his apartment after a night of partying. His sister did not make it back in the taxi she was supposed to have been in (we had all split up in, like, three taxis.) Turns out she had decided to go off with another guy first. Calle called her and yelled, angry that his little sister would go off alone with a guy in the city without his permission. Eventually she came back, and he was able to go to sleep.

Chapter 14

"The only way of catching a train I ever discovered is to miss the train before."

&G.K. Chesterton

Living in Sweden made it easy to travel around not only Sweden but also to other Scandinavian and Baltic countries. I took a train to Denmark, a ferry to Finland, drove to Norway with my mum. My sister got to go to Latvia, and my mum went to Estonia – I missed out on those. I've done plenty of travelling, but Scandinavia is by far my favourite area to do so.

As a family, we travelled up to the Lapplands to Kiruna and Jukkasjärvi. We took an overnight train that had a movie theatre carriage (I had never heard of such before), and a glass ceiling carriage so that one could watch the Northern lights, as they became visible.

We did a fair few activities up there, but the main attraction was the Ice Hotel. They build it with a new design every year. They also built an Ice Chapel that many people would come up to get married in. In the hotel, there was an Ice Bar with glasses made from ice and large Absolut label ice "posters" on the wall. There were ice chandeliers hanging in the halls and ice chairs around the lobby.

The rooms were all constructed differently. The honeymoon suite that year was Viking themed and the bed was shaped into a large Viking ship with seating at one end and shields on the wall. Every single thing in the rooms were made of ice except the reindeer pelts on top of the beds, and the backlighting that would shine through the ice. It was a magical place.

We stayed at the hotel for two nights. The family split up and we each stayed in the actual hotel for one night, and a heated cabin on the other. Thank goodness. I love the snow, but sleeping in it all night was a bit much!

The hotel provided arctic sleeping bags to sleep in, and as the concierge took us to our room, she told us a story of a guest from the year before. She said there had been a Scottish man that had come up, thought he was tough, and refused the sleeping bag – opting to sleep in only his boxers with the reindeer pelt. The hotel did wake up calls with warm lingon berry juice for the guests. She said that she and another employee decided to go to his room together – they were afraid they'd be finding a dead body! But the man got up in good spirits and they were so relieved. I, on the other hand, fully intended to use my sleeping bag to the most of its potential.

While up there we also went dog sledding. From the Ice Hotel there were a couple tourist dog sledding outings, but my dad wanted to do "the real thing." He tracked down a guy that would do longer distance sledding trips. In this arrangement instead of having everything already ready and taken care of; it was a lot more hands on with the dogs – helping to tie them, etc, as well as driving the sled yourself. We took two sleds, so the guy drove one as my dad drove the other. I have never been a huge dog person, so I was not necessarily excited about all the hands on part. But at least I can mark it all down to experience.

We then went on a long ride, took a couple hours if I remember correctly, over the frozen tundra. We came to the banks of an only partially frozen river where we tied to dogs up and got into a small boat to cross over. From the other side, we hiked through the snow – being careful not to misstep as any soft section would send us falling into waist deep fluff.

We eventually made it to his cabin. It was a Lapplandish style one room hut that was dug into the ground. After this long, cold journey we sat in this warm little dirt-walled hovel and ate fresh reindeer stew. This was the best part of the trip.

৪০০৪

Another standout family trip was when we went to Denmark. This is partially because I met a man there, and we ended up dating for a little while.

This trip started out in København or Copenhagen. I don't remember many of the actual activities there, but I recall it as one of my favourite cities. At eighteen I appreciated the classic old Scandinavian architecture, the history, the shopping... the ridiculously good looking Danish male population. Phew! I had thought Swedish boys were attractive!

We then travelled to Billund to go to Legoland. I mean, you can't go to Denmark without going to see the birthplace of the most world famous toy, can you?

While at Legoland, a pirate attacked me. A Danish pirate, er, um, theme park actor jumped out from behind something and started poking me with his foam sword. Apparently, this was enough for me to give up my contact details. He also gave me his. He was twenty-five then and his name was Sven Nielsen. I thought this was secretly amusing as my best friend, Svea, sometimes had to use her step-dad's last name of "Nilsson" – so it was like he was the Danish male counterpart of my Swedish female best friend. Okay, I know. I am amused by stupid things, ha ha.

After I went back home, Sven and I started to get to know each other by being pen pals and talking on the phone. We were pretty much having a long distance relationship after a while. He asked me to go stay with him for a while over school vacation. I arranged the tickets and hopped a train to Denmark.

This was the worst train ride of my life. I was so stressed out. There was a creepy guy that kept flirting with me on the overnight train to Malmö, and it made me uncomfortable to sleep. Then we stopped for two hours in the middle of the night, just outside of Jönköping, because someone had jumped in front of the train and committed suicide. This made me very late.

I called Sven right before I got on the commuter train in Malmö, luckily those crossed the bridge into Denmark every ten minutes or so. Also lucky I called when I did, because I hadn't realized my phone plan didn't cover out of country service. When I got to København, I had missed my next real train – luckily they let me on the next one that was leaving, but I had to sit on the floor.

Eventually I made it to Vejle. I had told Sven I would call him when I got on the last train, but since my phone didn't work I had to buy a public phone card as soon as I got off. Luckily for me, he had decided to go ahead and start the thirty minute drive to get me already. I was relieved... and so, so tired.

When I remember meals with Sven, I remember a lot of meat and beer. The first thing he did after he picked me up was to take me to a pub called kødhuset or something like that – literally *the meat house.* I'm not sure if it was because I had just finished my harrowing journey, or what, but it was really good. I remember at another restaurant we had ribs and beer. He ordered for us and - I wish I had a picture of this - it must have looked quaint as we sat together. He had the man's plate and I had whatever they called the small version. The same beer mugs, but mine was about one-third the size of his. I wondered if that made him feel manly.

Over the week we did various things around town. My parents would be horrified to learn I slept with him in his bed. I met his parents and his grandparents. They seemed lovely but, even though I knew Danish well enough in written form, I could not understand when they spoke to me.

He took me to the year closing festivities for Legoland. As an employee he got us the inside 'treats' like the last ride on one of the rollercoasters, and to be able to get up on the roof of the castle to watch the fire works. I didn't tell him that fireworks scare the hell out of me. I stood there with my eyes closed, his arm around me, pretending that there were no fire works exploding almost directly overhead. I clenched my fist, willing myself to stand still and not run. He was happy and thought he was making me happy, and I did not want to ruin that. I also didn't want to be the partypooper and make him leave if he wanted to be there with his friends. A few days later I admitted my fear of fireworks to him. He connected the dots, and his response translated to "Darling, why didn't you tell me?"

Eventually the week came to an end and he took me back to Vejle to catch my train. On the platform we said goodbye. As I was about to step on the train, he grabbed my wrist. I turned and he kissed me. He told me he loved me.

I felt sick to my stomach. I rode home (thank goodness in a seat this time) with my anxiety mounting. He *loved* me? I wasn't sure I could handle that! I was only eighteen. Maybe if my mind had been clouded by love, I wouldn't have thought that, but I was not in love with Sven. I felt like a jerk for feeling that way.

Even so, we still communicated as before. Eventually he also came up to Stockholm to stay with me for a few days. My parents, of course, put us in separate rooms – as if that really stops anything.

I remember taking him out to hang with friends at a bar – he was not impressed with the Storstark ("Big strong" beer), he thought Danish beer was better. I must say, actually,that my favorite beer is a Danish one so I guess he had a valid point. Afterwards we went and spent the night at a hotel.

Before I took him to his train, he kneeled in front of me in my kitchen and started to sing. I was so embarassed, not least of all because my sisters poked their heads around the corner and smirked as their faces disappeared again. I hadn't the heart to stop him though, so I let him continue to sing "I'm leaving on a tra-ain, don't know when I'll be back again..." Oh so cheesy, I know.

I don't remember exactly when he started talking about marriage – if it was this trip or if it was after. But eventually it was brought up. We hadn't been seeing each other all that long in my mind. However; I had also missed a period at this point. I said something about it to him, so he wouldn't be taken off guard. It also made me think I should at least consider it. I told him I would think about it.

Thank God it was a false alarm. I now knew the sweet relief of a pregnancy false alarm. Even so I considered the proposal a little longer. Eventually I decided I just didn't love him the same way he seemed to love me. I decided that even though I would love to live in Denmark, I wasn't so sure I wanted to be stuck in the small town of Billund. Sven worked for Legoland in summer and Lego factory in winter. His parents worked for

Lego, his grandparents retired from Lego. God bless Lego, but I did not want to be a Lego wife. I told him no.

Chapter 15

"My idea of good company...is the company of clever, well-informed people, who have a great deal of conversation; that is what I call good company.' 'You are mistaken,' said he gently, 'that is not good company, that is the best."

∞Jane Austen,
Persuasion

As I am writing all of my old memories, I keep wanting to use the phrase "back in the day." I think perhaps this is now the time to go ahead and use this phrase as I start to write about some other good friends from Sweden that were not associated with my school.

Back in the day, I used to hang out with a group of friends a lot, and it was almost always innocent fun and shenanigans. It's about time I talked about some of that, huh? I met the American sisters Elizabeth and Kristy through church, and we would get together for what was initially a Bible study time with a couple other guy friends. Eventually it kind of side tracked from that main purpose, and we just had a whole lot of fun. When we did do Bible study like activities that would last maybe an hour? I don't remember exactly, but considering there were several times we all stayed up together till about 7AM, the Bible study was a small part of our get togethers. In the group was also Luke, a Swedish guy who had been to University in the US for an exchange program and came back having had a love affair with everything American. He insisted on speaking in an American accent and even giving an American twang to his Swedish. His room was covered in American flags, including his bedclothes. Calling himself "Luke" instead of "Lukas." Next of the main group was Will. Not sure why he preferred Will, his real name was Vilhelm which is the Swedish form of William... so that's where the reasoning came in. He wasn't in love with an English speaking country like Luke was, but we called him Will anyway. After a while Luke brought along a friend named Rick. He was a music producer and had used to be a pop star himself. Pretty quickly Rick fell into our group and that makes the main characters of these stories. We occasionally had other friends around, but these were the people that were always there.

I remember a lot more about Elizabeth and Kristy as I also did a lot more with them outside of this group. In Sweden, you pick a major, or a "line," that you study starting in Gymnasium years. Beth went to school to study dance. She was so graceful and so often filled with joy. I remember her writing poetry in a journal a lot. We would compare poetry and comment on each other's work. I remember one day we were to meet up and we had both cut our hair short. We didn't tell each other what we had done hoping to surprise the other. When I opened my door we both screamed. She is also the friend that went with me when we got our ear cartilage pierced, and I got my other second hole pierced at the same time. She told me the cartilage wouldn't really hurt. I screamed an expletive in the beautician's face when the earring went in. Trust me. So much pain, much more than the ear lobe. She also gave me her old jazz shoes when I started to take jazz dance lessons at the Balletakademi, and they fit just right. Hmm, I miss Beth.

Kristy was the younger of the two. Beth was slightly older than me, and Kristy was slightly younger than me. She went to a school for music. She had a real talent for composing and singing. I remember she went with me to some function at the Embassy once. At the end of the night she sat down at the piano and started to play a song she had just written. I don't remember exactly what it was about, but as she started to sing I had to excuse myself to the bathroom. Her storytelling ability along with her beautiful voice was enough to bring tears to my eyes. I did not want the Marines to see me cry. I went to enough Marine parties that I knew I would see them again and they did not need that visual of me. Kristy's talent is probably one reason that Rick ended up dating her. Either that or because she was a hot blonde.

On the note of Rick, he and I used to text all the time with poetic blurbs back and forth. We would answer each other with almost nonsensical "poetry." But at the time it seemed so beautiful the things we would say. Once he asked me if I had ever written a song, he thought I would have the talent for it based off of these text conversations. I highly doubt that. I'm fairly good with words, but not so much the relating it to music. To get an idea of the type of stuff we would write, listen to "Fireflies" by Owl City. Later when this song came out it reminded me of Rick and I had wondered if he had written it, remembering our conversations. I know that he has written several English language pop songs that someone reading this probably has heard, so it was not out of the realm of possibility. So I looked it up, but didn't see his name attached anywhere so I guess it is just a coincidence. I wish I still had the notebook that I would record these texts in. I lost that in Hurricane Katrina, unfortunately.

಑಑಑

Our group's shenanigans usually were not planned much. We just would get together, usually at Will's house or when the girls lived in a big old Victorian home at one point we went there a bit. We would do dinner of some sort, or snack through the night, had some wonderful and oh-so-deep conversations. I wish I could remember more of exactly what was discussed, but I guess that is lost in the sands of time. We would watch silly movies and play fight. I remember one time we went to the video store, yes there were still VHS videos in use then, and we were trying to agree on a movie. Will and I were butting heads about it; Kristy – who had come with us – stepped out saying for us to work it out ourselves. He wanted *Charlies Angels*, the movie not the show. I told him it was obviously a stupid movie. He didn't believe me, and being taller and an older boy, he held it out of my reach as he pushed me back and ran the transaction real quick.

That night we watched it and after it was over he turned to me and said "That's the stupidest movie I have ever seen."

"I *TOLD* you that you wouldn't like it!"

"Well, you didn't tell me it would be *THAT* bad!!"

"I did *TOO!*"

He glared at me and then playfully pushed me over as he got up to walk out of the room.

"Now we have learned to listen to Rae, haven't we?" I murmured under my breath.

WHACK! A pillow, out of nowhere straight into my face!

Gosh, I had such a crush on Will. Ha ha. He was super smart and in University already by the time I was in Year 2. I remember going to his house to have him help me with my calculus. He had a really patient way of teaching me and made it easier to understand – though God help me if I had to try to do it again now. I also remember playing Kubb with him in his back yard after a study session, him using the same bigger boy trick to push me out of the way and not let me knock over his blocks. Then he ran over and kicked over all of mine! That's *not* how you play, Will!

Kristy recently reminded me of something that happened at one of these get togethers, and I thought it was a good example of me and my personality. One time when we were all at Will's house, he was sitting on his couch. I came running up behind, leaped over the couch and landed right next to him. I grabbed him and said "Stop making me want you!" Kristy said she remembers his face and it was priceless.

I was pretty much telling him the truth, but disguising it as a joke. I did that a lot. The theatre kid in me helped me to overcome certain attributes that held me back from saying and doing what I really wanted to sometimes. I used these desires as roles that I could hide behind and pretend it's just me being silly. I also really enjoyed making my friends laugh, and boy did they laugh at that. Swedish boys are pretty reserved and aren't always sure how to handle such forward behaviour. I knew it would be hilarious and I just went for it.

৪০৪

I remember walking down Sveavägen, a big main road in Stockholm, with Beth while trying to meet up with someone, Will, I think? Maybe it was someone else, but there were supposed to be a handful of people wherever we were going. I think it had to do with a church youth thing. Anyway, we could not find this stupid place he had described to us. We were laughing hysterically the whole way, and kept walking really far past and then having to turn around only to pass it again. At one point we found where we were supposed to turn off, and saw a car parked with someone in it. We thought it must be him, so we were laughing and carrying on as we would do, and went up as if to knock on the window when we suddenly realized it wasn't the right car. This started a whole new fit of giggles, I'm sure we appeared drunk. As we started to walk away, we looked back and the guy was looking at us and slowly reached over and locked his doors. This was the straw that broke the camel's back. We were on the pavement laughing. Sigh, fun times.

Eventually we found where we were supposed to be. The only other thing I remember from that night was that there was a guy named Kenny there. This is a really random memory and I'm not even sure why it sticks in my head and why I remember his name even. Anyway, someone offered up brownies to Kenny and he declined saying in English as he pointed to his face "I have a gum in my head." HAHAHA I was about to have a breakdown. Kenny, you cannot use funny English near a girl who had only just recovered from a laughing fit. Seriously.

৪৩ঌ

I remember going to some Walpurgis fires in town with at least Will and Beth. I remember I had promised them I would quit smoking. I had been doing pretty good about it, usually when I quit I could do it cold turkey and be off of it for a while with no issues, just the drinking or a major stressor would make me crave one. I remember this one Walpurgis I had a major stressor and his name was Dan. We all know at this point what kind of stressor he was, so I won't explain much about him here.

I had already bitten off all of my nails. This had been a nervous habit of mine since childhood, but at about twelve years old I had stopped and started having really long, lovely nails as a teenager. I would bite my nails all off without even thinking about it when something major was going on with Dan. I remember this happening at least two or three times, but I digress. I had bitten off all of my nails, so now I had nothing else to do for my nervous habit except pick up that pack of cigarettes again.

I slowed my pace just slightly so that Will and Beth came out ahead of me, and I slipped the cigarettes out of my pocket. I was about halfway through with one when Beth turned around and saw it. She gasped.

"Rachel! Drop it! Drop it now!"

Will stopped and turned as well.

I held my cigarette out to the side as she tried to bat it from my hand, and as I did I told them why I needed it.

"Come on you guys, it's just one… and Dan…"

Smack! My cigarette was on the pavement.

I defiantly pulled out another one and as I struggled to light it, Will snatched my pack from me and Beth grabbed the cigarette. They both started running. I started to run too and then decided I didn't want to run for a pack of cigarettes. Not least of all because even if I did catch up with them, Will was that bigger taller boy still. I was not going to degrade myself by engaging in a game of "keep away."

I called out to them "Okay, okay! *FINE.* I won't smoke, just wait up you guys!"

Chapter 16

"One of the things that binds us as a family is a shared sense of humour."

∞Ralph Fiennes

Our stuga, or cottage, in Sweden was a very quaint stereotypical home. It was a typical wood slat house, painted yellow with a white trim. It was a three story stuga on a street of almost identical stugas – though some were painted the other stereotypical colour of red.

We lived at number seven Ceremonimästarsvägen on the island of Lidingö. Lidingö is a suburb of Stockholm, one of the nicer areas of town. It had a law restricting any further building to maintain its beautiful natural scenery. There were gorgeous waterfront views, amongst a lush green interior.

When we first got to our house the person that took us there and showed us around commented to my parents, with typical Swedish attitude, that the large room on the bottom floor that had a door to the outside would be perfect for me. At my age, I would need an outside door to be able to come home in the middle of the night without disturbing the rest of the family. My parents then decided that room would be perfect for themselves.

I actually got another room on the bottom floor that ended up being perfect for me. My room didn't have any windows, which was perfect for my teenage sensibilities of coming home to sleep after school. I also had a linoleum floor and a mini kitchen like area. I had a full size fridge and freezer that I could keep my own special foods or alcohols in and a cabinet and counter space with a sink on one end of the room. This was perfect for when I wanted to paint. I would sit cross legged on the linoleum, painting my canvases with a sink nearby to rinse out my brushes, and plenty of cabinet space to store all of my extra supplies.

The second floor was the main living area that had the front door, as you walked in to the left was the small laundry area that segued into the garage. Next was the stairwell on the left, to the right was the entrance of the kitchen. If you went straight ahead you would get into the living room and dining room areas – with another door to the kitchen at one end. The house was typically decorated in the Swedish fashion with pale woods, white laminate, and iron fixtures.

The top floor is where all my sister's rooms were, along with a bathroom, spare room, and a large common room that housed the extra TV and the communal internet-computer.

I recall going to Anneke's side of the island and walking to a pier near her house to hang out by the beach with her and Elena on mild summer days. I remember sitting on the pebble covered bank on the Stockholm side with Dan, looking out over the water and the harbour as ships and ferries passed by. I also frequently went to Lidingö Centrum (the middle of 'town') to shop a little with my sister or to walk over to Elena's house with Anneke. I also remember going to the golf course with my family during winter where they had a huge hill to sled down.

৪৩

While living here, my sister Sarah got into a lot of trouble. Her new found freedom (thanks to the public transportation pass she had to have for school) found her the ability to get all over the city whenever and wherever she wanted to be. Unfortunately she found friends that introduced her to drugs and sex. She was only fourteen and at one point apparently sleeping with a twenty-five year old. She would worry my parents by leaving, not answering her phone, and not coming home for two days. She also came home once in a police car. My mum and her friend took her to a youth mental hospital at one point and that scared her out of her behaviour – temporarily.

Even with her erratic and out of control behaviour, I remember some really fun times with her. She and I hadn't been close as younger kids as we are four years apart, but once we both got to teenager hood, we became much closer.

Sarah and I liked to play tricks on each other. I remember mostly things that I did to her because, naturally, my tricks were much more hilarious.

One time I went upstairs and discovered that she was in the bathroom. I stepped up quietly and put my hand on the door handle, pulling it towards myself. As she tried to open the door, she got agitated, yelling at me to let the door go. Finally, as she made one strong tug, I let go. The door smacked her in the face and as she said "Ow!" the door slammed shut again.

I remember once we both decided to jump out and scare each other. As we leaped out and yelled out, we both scared each other so then we both started screaming in surprise, which then caused another surprise scream. We just stood there screaming at the top of our lungs until we broke down in a fit of giggles.

One of my favourite torments was when I had been up in Sarah's room chatting. As I walked out of her room, I turned a Furby around. She had this Furby on a shelf by her door, facing the wall because it freaked her out. So, naturally, I turned it around to face the room as I walked out and down to my room. About thirty minutes later, after I had fully forgotten I had even done that, I heard a blood curdling scream followed by the stomp-stomp-stomp of Sarah running down both flights of steps. She appeared in my doorway, frantic. "Rachel! Did you touch my Furby!?"

I burst out laughing and said "Oh yeah, that was me."

She breathed a sigh of relief, and then glared at me. "You have to come up and dispose of it now."

I followed her upstairs, laughing. Her fear only mounting as I tried twice to toss it in the trash can and it bounced right back out again. Finally I stuffed it down and went back downstairs. What happened next -I don't think she believes it wasn't me – was that another Furby turned up to torment her. I maintain that it was probably the cat, but if Esther had been stealthily observing the previous events, I suppose it could have been her. Anyway, Sarah decided to lay on the couch up there and watch some TV, her long hair hanging over the side. She said she felt a tug on her hair and she turned around to see one of my other sisters' Furby. She was creeped out and ran into her room, shutting her door behind her. When she came out a little while later, the same Furby was sitting in front of her door. I'm relatively certain that this experience scarred her for life. She still can't handle Furbies.

୫୦୦୪

I've mentioned before that my dad did some acting work while we were in Stockholm. I had signed up with one of the agencies he worked through, but as a girl with stereotypical Swedish looks, I did not have any feature that made me stand out in the crowd of other female hopefuls. My dad did, however; have a leg up over other actors his age. He had the Swedish look, so he could be cast as someone who was supposed to be Swedish, but he also was an American so that helped when he needed to play an American character, and there was less of a pool to pull from in his gender and age group.

He started out doing several commercials. I must say that I find Swedish commercials very clever and usually pretty hilarious. First he did a series for a phone company; I believe it was for Teliasonera. In this series he played an office person that along with several other people worked inside a mobile phone. One showed the owner of a phone typing a text. Inside the phone you see people working and a manager shouting orders as several start running around, placing "pixels" where they were supposed to go. After a few in the series were aired, and the public had time to get to know the premise of the commercials, another one aired showing the offices with the cast falling all over the place and desperately holding onto desks as they screamed. Pan out to see a bored guy at work spinning his mobile.

He also did a commercial for manpower in which he played a disapproving older scientist. Then he took a job playing "Optiker Berglund" or "Optician Berglund." This character was mostly a print character, appearing in a comedy series for Spermaharen. They released a book and had a website for that character. At one point, Optiker Berglund also released a CD called "Optiker Berglund sings Randy Newman," and he posed for the CD

92

cover and there was a life size cardboard cut-out of him in stores advertising the CD. Then, he made the music video. He did a music video for the Randy Newman song "You've got a friend in me."

The only other project I recall was when he appeared in a movie for the Stockholm Film Festival. Unfortunately, I never got the chance to go to that festival and though he was promised a copy of it, it never arrived so I have not yet seen it. However; this movie was about Aliens landing in Sweden. Since Sweden had no real experience dealing with Aliens, the people in charge of the investigations had to call some agents from the USA to help them out. That would be because as Americans, we had so many incidents involving Aliens. My dad played one of the serious, gruff, American agents. A music video was also made from this movie, I did see that – but no clips of my dad ended up in that.

೮෪෫

While I am talking about my immediate family, I'll discuss a few family traditions. It's funny how you do things as a family and don't really consider them "traditions," until you move out and have to make them cohesive to what your partner considers the correct way to do things.

For Christmas there are a few things that stick out in my mind. We had little traditions that evolved over the years; such as opening one present on Christmas Eve, opening our stockings first – always finding an orange in the toe. My Grandma would always send each grandchild a Christmas ornament to be opened at Thanksgiving. These were themed for each child – my sisters got rabbits, mice, and cats respectively. My theme was bears. We always knew which ones were ours and we had a readymade stock of ornaments once we moved out of the house and had our own trees. Even now my Christmas is decidedly bear centric – I even found myself a teddy bear angel tree topper several years back. Now my mother has taken up this tradition for my kids… it was nice for several years having only bears on my tree, but now they occupy space with cats and dogs.

We would leave cookies out for Santa, and a couple carrots out for the reindeer. Santa would always answer our note telling us how delicious it all was and how much he and the reindeer enjoyed it. He would have special handwriting that included candy canes drawn throughout the script. As we got immersed in the Swedish culture we started to leave out *risgrynsgröt* (rice porridge) with cardamom and cinnamon for *Tomten*. Tomten means "The Gnome," and though it is synonymous now with "Santa," it also refers to other gnomes, including the house gnome that is the head of the gnome family that lives on your property. This is a belief/tradition that comes from the farming communities back in the day. The idea is that Tomten helps to protect your farm, and helps out around the property – keeping animals safe, etc. He loves risgrynsgröt, and is appeased for the year if you honour him by remembering to leave some out for his Christmas Eve feast. We also followed the tradition of placing the seven candle candelabras in the windows and leaving them lit till about February. Of course by this day and age, they were electric. I loved walking through town this time of year – with the city becoming dark before I even got out of school, it just felt cosy walking through the snowy streets seeing these lights in just about every window.

Another tradition started in Sweden was that my dad started to celebrate our birthdays by taking us out for a dinner and a movie of our choice. I believe it was because he started to feel out of touch with teenage girls and wasn't real sure what to get us – let alone our tastes were probably getting more expensive by then. Even so, I enjoyed my dad dates on my birthdays.

Easter is another big traditional family holiday. As young girls, we would always get a new dress and go to church. I don't remember when we started not getting the dresses, but I suppose we eventually got too old to care about that. We always had the same baskets year after year. Our Easter baskets were shaped like eggs with each sister having her own specific colour. We would come out to discover the Easter Bunny had filled them with goodies and small presents. Then we would look around for eggs he had hidden, usually in the house. When we were visiting

Grandparents that time of year, the Bunny would use these fancy bunny baskets that had different colour ribbons around the necks corresponding to each sister and cousin. The trick here was that the Bunny didn't hide the eggs, he hid the baskets instead.

Thanksgiving is probably my favourite time of year because, well, food. My dad has always been a really good cook. My mum is too, but my dad's skills exceeded hers. He would spend two days cooking. Usually making at least four pies the day before – two pecan, two pumpkin. We would also have such staples as green bean casserole, mashed potatoes, cranberry sauce, and of course turkey. Usually we drank non-alcoholic sparkling cider, but as I got legally old enough to drink in Sweden my parents poured up champagne if I so cared. Christmas had no such specific menu, though we often ate corned beef and cabbage as it was a family favourite and not so cheap that we ate it often. I do remember my dad often making these brownies with a mint sauce on top and homemade egg nog. As we got to Sweden, we would drink glögg, a hot spiced wine often mixed with Vodka or Aquavit for adults, and the additions of blanched almonds and raisins.

My parents loved to entertain, so we often had people over for dinners for these special occasions. Once in a while we'd go to other dinner parties. Since my dad was a diplomat, he had several diplomat friends and co-workers. It was only natural that this would be a big part of my childhood.

<u>Chapter 17</u>

*"I may not have gone where I intended to go, but I think
I have ended up where I needed to be."*

*&Douglas Adams,
The Long Dark Tea-Time of the Soul*

As Graduation time neared, my mum came back to Sweden to be there as well as help me pack and get ready to go back to the States. As a graduation present she also took me on a trip to Norway. I am pleased to say I got to see every Scandinavian country while I lived in Sweden. They may all squabble amongst themselves and make jokes about each other as if they are siblings, but they have a lot in common. Not least of all that they are beautiful countries that I would love to go back to one day.

Graduation in Sweden is just plain fun. For several weeks in the spring you attend various *studentskivas* which are parties for various graduating friends or groups. For mine I just invited my three best friends over for a nice meal, Svea, Anneke, and Maja. Maja, however; was grounded and couldn't make it. That girl was grounded so much!

For weeks the various schools in town do their graduation days on different days. If they didn't, there would be chaos in the town. My graduation was pretty typical and it went like this: my class met along with several other classes in a park near the school to have a champagne breakfast. Eventually we made our way to the school to get our graduation class picture taken and then go into the auditorium so that the principal could give a speech, we all sang, and drank at that time as well. Then lining up by class, the girls dressed in white and the boys in suits – and all of us wearing the sailor style graduation hats – we did our *utspring* or running out of the building into the courtyard to waiting friends and family. We sang and chanted – chanting things like "ES3b! ES3b!" and "Vi Tar Studenten, na na na na na!"

After this goes on for a little while you meet up with friends and family that are holding a big sign with your name and class written on it – along with a baby/young child picture of yourself. You get flowers and stuffed animals tied to blue and yellow ribbon hung around your neck, and then make your way to your transportation. Most kids gather in groups to chip in and get flatbed trucks that get decorated. Some may only go around a couple at a time in a regular car. I was in a group that hired a truck. Drinking and singing continued as you drove around town showing off to everyone that you have taken *studenten* (graduated/taken grad exams).

After a while you usually gather at home with friends and family for dinner and a party. Since most of my family wasn't around, Svea invited me to hers. So that is where I went after I climbed off of the truck in the middle of town because the alcohol had caught up with me and I was desperate to pee.

ಙೞ

Shortly after graduation, I moved back to Virginia. This time to Williamsburg where the rest of my family was. During the summer, I spent quite a bit of time road tripping around Virginia with Svea as she had come to stay with her step-brother at his house in Roanoke.

I had gotten into a few Universities. Including William & Mary. Looking back now, I wish I had chosen William & Mary!! But I chose Longwood. Longwood was about a four hour drive from my parent's house. I chose to start in the theatre program, planning on adding a backup minor later and Longwood had more minors that interested me at the time.

Longwood was not what I expected. First off, it bugged me that when you are choosing the college and your parents are there, they go on and on about how safe it is. On our first day of orientation, with parents safely at home, they start telling us that Longwood was statistically one of the worst schools on the east coast for rape. I did not feel unsafe there, but it bothered me that they would lie to my parents like that.

After several days I decided to go to a party with my roommate. She was a nice enough girl, and now that I was relatively settled I thought I should make myself get out there and make more friends. This frat party was the most juvenile thing I had ever witnessed. It was all about getting the chance to drink. The house was hot and stifling and there was a long line just waiting for the keg.

In Sweden you can start drinking pretty much as young as you like, as long as your parent approves. Most of the time that is around sixteen years old. At eighteen you can buy your own liquor at grocery stores and by the glass at bars. When you are twenty you can by the hard stuff by the bottle at the state run liquor store.

This keg did not impress me. At nineteen, I was not feeling the need to go out and get trashed on warm beer just because I was finally out of Mummy and Daddy's house. I had basically been living away from home for several months before then. I tried to make a go of it as far as meeting people and stepped outside to chat with some classmates. Then one of the frat guys came around to usher everyone back in because the police were circling the block, looking for underage drinkers. It was not worth it to me to have to go back inside that stifling, sweat smelling house, so I walked back to my dorm instead.

In class we were treated like children. This was new to me. I wasn't sure I appreciated that. In Kungsholmens I was an adult. I was responsible for myself and my studies. Here I was a kid that needed to be introduced to adult living. I understand, in a way, why it was like that – most of my classmates were a year or two younger, and had been treated that way in their own High Schools. They were the kids that OHMYGOSH just had a beer (don't tell my parents!) They didn't notice what I noticed. I felt talked down to and degraded in this atmosphere.

However; I was also being actively recruited for the Marine ROTC (Reserve Officer Training Corps.) The recruitment officer even took my mum and me out for lunch and he was really pleased with my background. That was interesting and I was actually seriously considering the Marine Corps at that time. Though I didn't follow through, mainly because my next school did not have that program and then I got married.

I might have stuck it out a little longer had it not been for the financial issue. At first I was only granted $250 and a Federal work-study placement. My dad wrote back to FAFSA and let them know that he had actually retired and was not making nearly as much money as he was the year before. He told them that I would need to pay my own way. They lowered my grant to $150.

At Longwood there was a rule that freshman could only work in the cafeteria. Fine, whatever – except this was only a College work-study job. Under the stipulations of the Federal work-study I was not allowed to take a College work-study job. I applied for a Federal one in the admissions office. It was the only Federal one open at the time. They were impressed with me and asked when I could start. Then she realized I was a freshman. I was not allowed to work there because freshmen worked in the kitchen. What in the actual fuck.

I looked for a job in the small town; only thing I could find was a bookstore that offered me two hours a week on Tuesdays.

After three weeks or so, I packed up and I went home.

Too late to accept William & Mary, I went to community college. It was a lot cheaper, I could get a lot of basics out of the way and they treated me like an adult. That was good enough for me.

Chapter 18

"Reader, I married him."

&*Charlotte Brontë,*
Jane Eyre

Even though I was living in Williamsburg, I started to see Andre again. He had emailed me out of the blue during my senior year and we had started getting to know each other again. Andre was still in Frederick, so during the summer I would drive up to spend a week with him here and there and he would come down a couple of times to see me in Virginia.

We dated for nearly four months this time. At one point in Frederick we got caught in a rainstorm while we were out at the park. At first we ran for cover into the clamshell – a covered amphitheatre that was there. After a moment, I thought "Oh, what the hell?" and dragged him back into the rain and we danced around with our arms raised and our faces basking in the raindrops. I would recommend anyone dance in the rain at least once in their life.

I thought maybe I could love him. But the distance got to be a bit much, especially once school started up. We broke up. He wanted to be friends; at that point I wasn't so sure I could actually do that.

ಹಾ ಗ

I was working at the DoD base my mum worked at. I was a security person. I worked with a lot of older people. At community college there were also hardly any people my age. It was hard to meet people and I was a little lonely. I started looking online through match.com and kiss.com, not necessarily for a relationship – though that would be nice – but also for some friends my age. First I met Brandon. We went on a date. He was nice. We were not attracted to each other, but he invited me to go bowling with a bunch of friends and I almost instantly had a handful of new friends. We all met up nearly weekly and it was nice to have a group I felt included in.

Next I met Chase. He was a photographer in the Navy. He was muscular and good looking. He said he liked me and was interested in a relationship. He ended up being a jerk and I didn't have the patience to wait around for him. A few months later, after I was already in another relationship he called to tell me he was moving to England and was going to make over $80,000 a year. He said I must feel bad I didn't give it a proper go with him. What an ass. Even if we had, I would only have known him for three months. I doubt I would have moved for him.

I was getting nasty messages from guys on these sites – like the guy that was engaged, but was looking for some fun on the side. Ick. I decided to let the month's subscription run out. Two days before that ended, I got a message from another Navy guy. He had just gotten back from a deployment. I gave him my email address so we could bypass the site.

We emailed for several weeks, he started using babelfish to translate his emails into Swedish for me. I thought it was cute that when he signed his name "Meadows," babelfish would translate it to "Ängar" and he would leave it that way.

Eventually he gave me his phone number and asked me to call him. I had been playing it safe and wouldn't release mine first. He was surprised when I called him. Another few weeks of phone calls and we decided to meet. He lived an hour and a half away, so we met nearly half way at a Don Pablos. He was shorter than I expected, I was more bohemian than he expected.

After that we went on several double dates over the course of a couple weeks. He and his roommate, Jeff, would come to Newport News or Williamsburg to take me and my friend Leyla out. Jeff and Leyla would conspire – she would tell Jeff what I would say about Jason. She told Jeff I didn't like Jason's moustache. Jeff told Jason "Dude. Shave, she hates it."

After a few weeks Jason asked me to be his girlfriend. He was a nice guy and all, but I wasn't really attracted to him. I told him "Let's just keep hanging out and be friends." He said "Don't say 'let's be friends,' I've heard that before and it never works out." He denies this now, but he then asked me to date him for two weeks and then make a decision. Whatever I decided after two weeks, he would respect.

Two weeks flew by and he asked me again. I said "What the hell, it's been fun. Sure I'll keep dating you." At Christmas he took me home to North Carolina to spend it with his family.

After that, I spent most weekends at his apartment in Virginia Beach.

℘ℭ

On July 4th, 2003, Jason came over. We were going to go out and do dinner and a movie or something like that. We went to my room to check the newspaper listing. He started hemming and hawing, said he wanted to talk about something with me.

He said "As you know, I am getting an early out from the Navy, and …well… I've been thinking. You know, I got a job in Louisiana and well, I was thinking…and thinking… and then I thought…."

"*Yeeees*?" I prompted him

"Please don't interrupt! … So I was thinking and thinking, and well, I don't know anyone in Louisiana… so I was thinking…"

"Uh, huh." I said, smirking at his nervousness.

"Well, I was thinking that maybe… if you want to… you could come with me, I mean at least I know you …and we have fun… but then I was thinking… that you should be an honest woman if you move away with me… soooo…. Will you marry me?"

I said yes.

He wanted to be old fashioned and "ask for my hand." My dad wasn't home, so he made me stay in my room as he went and sat my mum down in the living room and told her what was happening and asked her permission. My mum sat in shocked silence for a minute. To ease the tension, and because it was my mum's birthday the next day, Jason said (with jazz hands no less) "Haaapppy Biiirthdaaay!"

104

Jason had to be at his new job in just over four weeks. At first we planned to just go to the courthouse, but when we took my grandparents out for dinner the next day to tell them, they were upset that they wouldn't see me get married. We threw together a small backyard wedding for family and were married on July 18th. We had a quick weekend honeymoon in a nice hotel in Williamsburg, and then he had to ship off with the Navy for a week before he was released. When he got back we had just a couple days to finish packing and get down to New Orleans.

<u>Chapter 19</u>

*"You may not control all the events that happen to you,
but you can decide not to be reduced by them."*

∞Maya Angelou

Right after Jason and I were married, we moved to Metairie, Louisiana. This is a suburb of New Orleans. There is a reason the call it the "Dirty South." I was happy enough being married and living with Jason, but ugh. New Orleans is just not my favourite place.

I had a string of bad jobs. The jobs in themselves were not terrible, but there were people I worked with that were horrible and they seem to have an old boy's club in every establishment down that way. I did work part time at a retail store called Bath and Body Works that whole time and I did really enjoy it there. Every other full time job, however; was the pits.

After a year, we moved to another suburb and bought a house. Westwego was at least a nicer area. We got some dachshund puppies. I have never been a 'dog person,' but I loved my doxies anyway (I just didn't love their messes.)

Eventually around the beginning of 2005, Jason had to travel to Mississippi for work. They put him in an apartment and he was to stay for six months. During this time I would go visit every weekend, but still lived in Louisiana during the week. About four months in to this arrangement he got news that there would be a permanent transfer to Mississippi.

We put our house up for sale, I put in a transfer with Bath and Body Works and I moved out that way.

ಬುಡಿ

We rented a house while the other one stood on the market. I went to live with Jason full time again. If I remember correctly, this was around the time that I noticed Jason's seizures for the first time. Over the previous year, apparently, he had started to have partial seizures. They were affecting his face, and he had decided not to tell me about them. I think he was slightly embarrassed and just did not want me to worry and fuss over him.

We were in a department store when a clerk came up and asked if we needed help. Jason turned to him, his face screwed up like he was angry and he grunted at him. The guy just apologized for disturbing us and said he'd be at the counter if we needed him.

I said something to Jason about his behaviour. I was a retail clerk; you don't treat retail clerks that way even if they are annoying. Now Jason had no choice but to tell me what was going on. He had sleep studies and doctor visits, but no doctor in Mississippi could figure out what was wrong.

‟∞∢

We were only in Mississippi together for two months before Hurricane Katrina hit the Gulf coast. The weekend that it approached I told Jason we should probably leave. He said I was making a fuss. That Friday I had to work at JC Penney, we were starting to prep for the storm. I asked what the plan was for people who had weekend shifts. I was supposed to work Sunday morning, after all. They told me if they closed the store the scheduled personnel would get a call.

By Sunday morning I got no call, so I headed out to work. As I drove the two minute drive to the mall, I listened to the radio. The hosts were talking about the storm and advised everyone get out of town. It had turned to a class five hurricane and it was coming our way. I got to the mall; the entire thing was boarded up. The radio hosts told those that remembered Hurricane Camille from the 1960s that it would be a worse storm than that. They told those of us that weren't around then to trust them and get out of town. I went home and woke Jason.

Jason at first tried to brush me off, but then I turned on the news. He was convinced and we started to pack some bags. He tried to tell me to straighten up the living room. I asked him why we would waste time with that. He said if anyone had to walk through after the storm... I gave him a "really?" look. If there was a reason for anyone to walk through afterwards, the room would be in a much worse state.

I tossed all of my Swedish books, photos and yearbooks into a plastic container. I thought that would be good enough. Now I regret that I didn't just toss it in the back of the pickup with everything else. Luckily I grabbed my favourite Swedish book my dad had given me – Bröderna Lejonhjärta (The Brothers Lionheart) by Astrid Lindgren. I also grabbed my graduation cap and a couple little mementos from our wedding.

The dogs seemed to sense what was coming – as soon as I opened the kennel all four dogs that we had at that point marched single file into it. It was usually a struggle to get them into that thing.

We drove up to North Carolina to stay for a few days. Well, that was the plan anyway. The next day Hurricane Katrina hit the Gulf. We watched news reports they were claiming over inflated numbers of casualties in New Orleans at first, they were talking of the dead bodies, the people that were trapped, the animals screaming in the night from getting caught in downed power lines. They talked about all the people that either wouldn't or couldn't get out of the city. All I can remember after that was lying in bed, clutching my rosary and crying.

I remembered a mockumentary I had watched earlier in the year. It was about what would happen to New Orleans if a similar hurricane hit it the way Katrina did. It was spot on. When I watched it I had thought "when did this happen?" Then realized when it showed a "news" clip and had a date in the future of September 2005 that it was a mockumentary. Hurricane Katrina hit New Orleans on August 29, 2005. I saw this filmmaker on the news. Even he was surprised at how well he had predicted this natural disaster.

Luckily our house in New Orleans was on high enough land that it did not catch the storm surge. There was storm damage, but not so serious considering. We were lucky that now that the storm had happened and people could see it still stood, they wanted to buy it. At least that was one less worry.

The house that was a mile from the Mississippi coast however... This house was hit with the full blast of water. We lost just about everything. Including my plastic container that had been knocked over, lid coming off as it fell. FEMA and our insurance argued back and forth about whether it was a surge or a flood, because each would only pay for one and they wanted the other guy to have to pay. Eventually the insurance man upped and paid.

The day after the storm, our land lord called and said we had to come clean out our stuff immediately or he would toss everything on the street. We told him it would take a few days to arrange getting a trailer and getting down there. We had heard reports that only relief people were allowed past a certain point, and even that trailers were being commandeered for relief efforts as well. The land lord was entirely unreasonable. He tried to say it was within his right because we hadn't paid our rent yet. Our rent wasn't even due for another few days. Jason told him he'd be there by a certain date, and by the time he got off the phone he had no assurance that anything would still be there to sort.

He and his brother went down together. He told me he did not want me to go. I am honestly glad I didn't have to go and see everything up close. Some of our valuables were missing so at first Jason suspected the land lord. But when he went to stay with his best friend that night he discovered Hunter had gone and got it all for us just in case. I'm glad he was the one person we ever gave a key to. Hunter was in the Navy with Jason, and then joined up with the company a year after Jason did. He was in Louisiana and Mississippi with us. I was glad for Jason, who by then had started to become less sociable, to have a good friend so close.

My car had been flooded out so an insurance adjuster had to come check it out. By the time he made it, Jason was back in North Carolina. The adjuster called and told us our car wasn't there. He said we could still make a claim, but had to do a police report first. When the police called me back they said it was not in any junk yards. They said they interviewed neighbours and they believed that the land lord had taken it and sold it for parts. Unfortunately they had no proof to arrest him for it. Fortunately the insurance accepted the claim and sent us a check.

ಬಂಛ

There is only one other thing I want to mention about Hurricane Katrina. I mention it only because I was so grateful.

My phone rang the day after the storm. It was someone from The Limited corporate office. The Limited is a company that owns many retail stores, including Victoria's Secret, The Limited, Express, White Barn Candle Company... and Bath and Body Works.

They called "just to see if I was alright." They asked me if I needed any immediate assistance, housing or shelter. I told them that I was with family so I was okay on that front. I thanked them for their concern. The guy told me that they would be helping me out as much as they could, and once they figured it all out they would be in touch.

The Limited Corporation continued to pay me my average weekly pay of fifteen hours work for three months. They sent me a $500 lump sum check. They sent me $400 worth of gift cards to Victoria's Secret, The Limited, Express, and Bath and Body Works so I could start replenishing our clothes and body care items. They sent me a card that entitled me to 65% off at all of these stores for three months so that my gift cards would stretch further. I didn't need the housing assistance, but I know they helped other employees with that.

The Limited Corporation had always talked the talk when they said they cared for their employees. Now they proved they could walk the walk.

Chapter 20

"Sometimes you will never know the value of a moment until it becomes a memory."

&Dr Suess

Jason needed to get back to work, but the ship yard he worked at was trashed. The company was starting some layoffs. He was told he was too valuable to the company to get laid off, but Jason knew that I was too apprehensive to go back and he felt bad that someone else would have to lose their job anyway. He applied for a transfer hoping to spare at least one person's job.

As a temporary solution the company sent him to San Francisco to work on the same project in the office setting. Again we were separated for a bit as I stayed in North Carolina with his family. The company did pay for me to go up and stay with him for a week or so during this time which was nice, but otherwise I was with family.

During this time I got a part time job as a tax form proof reader. It was for a software company that prepped every State's yearly tax forms and also applied them to software applications. During the interview test I did not finish proof reading in the allotted time. I did, however; find the most mistakes anyone had ever found on the test, even without having finished. They offered me the job right away.

With that to keep me busy most days, I started to look for other activities for the rest of my time. My mother-in-law introduced me to a friend of hers that ran a theatre troupe. It had felt like so long since I had been involved with anything like that. They had started to rehearse *Once On This Island* and he asked me to help with special effects. I also lent a hand with making props and costumes as well. I had a blast. I remember Sean would get irritated that the lighting people had a hard time with their cues. The first time I sat down to the special effects control board for a rehearsal, I got everything correct and on cue. Sean came up and said in my ear "Please say you will be here for my next production." I laughed and said "I don't think..." He stopped me mid-sentence and said "Don't say you won't be here. Just pretend you will and that will make me happy."

ဆာလ

While in North Carolina, I spent a lot of my free time with Jason's Granny. I would walk up the hill just about every day and sit at her kitchen table as she reminisced to me over a glass of tea. Later, when we would go visit after her Alzheimer's started to take hold, she would tell me the same stories over and over again – having the same conversation four or five times in the space of an hour. In early 2010, we got news that she had been passing blood when she went to the bathroom. Jason's parents had taken her to the emergency department and they told her to come back in the morning when the correct doctor could see her. That night she fell and broke her hip. As soon as I heard that, I said to Jason "Granny is going to die."

He didn't agree, but I had a gut feeling. Alone, in my car, I cried over her impending death. I called my own grandmother and cried to her about it. Within the week she went into a coma and passed shortly after. Jason and Emma travelled over there to attend the funeral. I couldn't go because it coincided with my job start date at Vanderbilt Hospital.

Jason called me from North Carolina to tell me about when she had passed. I said "okay," very matter of fact. He thought I was an unfeeling bitch. He didn't know I try to avoid crying in front of him. I guard myself from showing emotions to men. He didn't know I had sobbed the week before or that I had already come to terms with her death earlier than he had.

ဆာလ

A transfer came through shortly after and Jason was sent to Clarksville, Tennessee. I quit my job, said my goodbyes and packed up my things and drove to meet him in December of 2005.

Chapter 21

"But then Jonathan said it was something he must do, even if it was dangerous. 'Why?' I wondered. 'Otherwise you're not a human being but just a piece of dirt' said Jonathan."

∞Astrid Lindgren,
The Brothers Lionheart

Tennessee is the place that I have lived the longest up to this point. We were there from December 2005 to January 2013. During this time I did a few different jobs. I worked at a daycare to start. That was alright, but I was not paid near enough for what I had to put up with. I did love the kids, however. I started with the pre-schoolers and then after I prepped them for their Kindergarten entrance tests, I was moved up to work with the school agers as an Art teacher.

After that I worked for a law firm. I thought maybe I could be interested in paralegal studies or something. It wasn't a bad line of work, except that I worked for an attorney that lauded his firm as the "Christian" firm in town. He was a deacon at the Baptist church. I thought it would be good to work for a Christian company. This man was not a Christian. He was a two faced bigot. He cheated his clients out of money every chance he had. His employment practices were questionable. I became fully aware of all this when I moved from reception to work as the Billing Manager. He was trying to screw over a former employee. At the time I didn't know who it was, but based on the circumstances I told them they could not do that and cited Federal law to them.

I very quickly was banished to a slow office elsewhere in town. I was targeted by the Office Manager and she started making my life as hard as she could. Soon after, I was fired. I found out right after who that employee had been. She reported them to the Tennessee government and told me about it. By this time they were also trying to screw someone else over. All three of us handed over all the information we had about his employment practices that were against the law. At the very least, this made his life very hard and he lost a lot of money. I still think he deserved worse, but at least it was something.

I did a little retail and I helped out a patent lawyer friend of mine occasionally. Eventually I started working at Fort Campbell Federal Union.

It was a pretty nice place to work and I was pleased with that. I stayed with them for about two years.

ະວ∞

Once in Tennessee, Jason's seizures got worse. It had started with facial seizures. His face would freeze, but he still knew what was going on and had control over the rest of his body. They became more frequent until he was having at least one a day. He stopped wanting to go out anywhere besides work because he was embarrassed.

Finally one day he had one and didn't realize it. He also started screaming at night. Sometimes wordless screams, sometimes they were filled with expletives. I couldn't sleep with him. I had taken to an air mattress in the spare room. I would try to stay with him on the weekends when I didn't have to worry about work in the morning. Most of the time I was in the guest room though. I had mentioned this to a couple friends, but they apparently they did not realize how bad it was. One friend came over one afternoon while Jason was napping. As we chatted he suddenly screamed from the bedroom and she actually jumped.

"What was that?!" She asked.

"It's Jason. I told you he does that when he's sleeping."

She said in surprise "Oh! You were serious!"

The doctors he saw in Clarksville could not figure it out. He suddenly started having full body grand mal seizures. His neurologist tried a few meds on him. They would work for a while and then he'd have a worse one than before. Every month or so they were increasing dosages. He had a bad seizure at work and called to make an appointment. He couldn't feel his arm. He went in the next morning and had one in front of her, as he came around his nose started to bleed. She decided that it was beyond her scope and sent him to Vanderbilt University Hospital to see a neurologist there. This doctor knew what was wrong. He had seen cases like Jason's before. It was a fairly rare condition. Rare enough that not all neurologists necessarily come across it in their career. Jason had Partial-Frontal Lobe Epilepsy. Jason had two choices: take meds for the rest of his life, steadily increasing them with no guarantee of the seizures stopping or he could have brain surgery and take out the localized area that was causing the seizures. At most he would just have to take his meds for some years after as he was very slowly weaned off of them, but he wouldn't have it for the rest of his life. Jason chose the surgery.

Chapter 22

"If I loved you less, I might be able to talk about it more."

&Jane Austen,
Emma

In Tennessee I started attending Beautiful Saviour Lutheran Church. I had started to be interested in Lutheranism years before, while in Sweden. I had discovered that a main patriarch of my family, Oskar Englund, the one who had ten children, half of whom moved to the US at the turn of the 20th Century – was a Lutheran priest in addition to his iron works job. He preached in a small church in Axmarsby. A tiny village, only slightly bigger than the village of Axmarsbruk that held the iron factory he worked in and lived by. I wondered if it was in my blood to be Lutheran. Later while in Mississippi and North Carolina, I had started to investigate Lutheranism.

Beautiful Saviour was a pretty little church on top of a hill. It is of the WELS synod, which is one of the most conservative synods in the US. I took the membership class and became a member. The pastor remembered my name after the first time meeting me. Remember when I talked about New Life and not feeling important to them because they couldn't remember my face? Pastor Green remembered my face. Years later when Jason had surgery, Pastor Green came to visit. This was the first time they had met. A year later Jason came to a special church service and Pastor Green remembered his name. When I didn't come on a Sunday, Pastor Green would notice I was missing from the 300-plus congregation. What a talent that is. I felt important and wanted in this church. I felt comfortable and at home.

A few things that drew me to the WELS synod is that they believe in the "Invisible Church." To us this means that you do not have to be Lutheran to go to Heaven. We believe that as long as you believe in Jesus as your Saviour, you will go to Heaven. Believe it or not, I have been to churches before that do not preach that. WELS, along with other Lutherans, has three main pillars of faith: Faith alone, Grace alone, Scripture alone. I also appreciated a study that Pastor Green had given me a copy of. This study broke down the differences between the American Lutheran Synods. It also had statistics based off of interviews with pastors from all three of the main synods – ELCA (Evangelical Lutheran Church of America), MLS (Missouri Lutheran Synod), and WELS (Wisconsin Evangelical Lutheran

Synod). The ELCA is very liberal, the Missouri Synod is conservative, and the WELS is even more so. What amazed me was that on various doctrinal beliefs, the ELCA and MLS reported that not all pastors believed or disbelieved the same things as their counterparts. Seeing the numbers for WELS pastors on those topics, however; showed always either 0% or 100% belief. Nothing in between. I liked that if I moved and went to a different WELS church, I could be assured of the doctrine I would be taught. I also liked that Pastor Green would break down his sermon and explain history to us. He would go back to the Hebrew or Greek, retranslate it and compare to the Bible he used. He would explain the words and the different connotations and deeper meanings they had. I felt like I really learned something, and that he was concerned with teaching the truth as best he could.

๚๛

Beautiful Saviour was where I met Dane. We taught Sunday school together. At the time he claimed he didn't have female friends. He found females around our age and younger as silly. He was not entirely misogynistic as he respected older women, mother like figures. But he had a bit of a chauvinist side. For some reason, we became friends anyway. Very quickly we were calling each other our respective best friend.

Dane and I started to do everything together. Movies, going to plays, eating out, he would even drop by my work occasionally to bring me lunch. By this time, my husband's epilepsy had become worse and he barely left the house except for work. He was happy to let Dane take me out to do things he didn't want to do anyway.

Eventually at home it got to a point that I did not want to be there if I didn't have to. It started with one of Jason's meds. It appeared to make him angry all the time, but even after the doctor took him off that med, the anger did not disappear. He became downright mean.

Because of all this, the not wanting to be home, I started spending even more time with Dane. At this time in his life he was ever the host and nearly every weekend he was hosting parties and BBQs. At these events there was always free flowing alcohol. It's where I went to forget. Once in a while the drinking would happen elsewhere, there were also a fair few Wednesdays that the group went out for drinks.

During this time my life felt dark. I will admit there were times I wondered what it would be like to be with Dane. Then he would say something asinine and sexist and I would decide that wouldn't be a good idea. He introduced me to a lady that had become a mother figure to him. In fact, he called her his "second mom." He wanted us to be friends. She was nice enough, but every time I would see her she would start telling me how much Dane needed me. She would tell me she could tell I was unhappy and that she thought I should get a divorce and marry Dane. I was honestly tempted, but no matter how unhappy I was I still wanted my marriage to work out. I was a Lutheran and I didn't believe in divorce (except in certain extenuating circumstances.) Deep down I still loved Jason and hoped it would get better. Eventually I cut her off because I knew I didn't need the temptation. It took me years to reveal that to Dane.

೩೦೦೩

This main group of friends were all Army officers. After all, that is what Dane was. In this group was a man named David.

I read an autobiography once where the lady went through a similar period to what I am about to write. In her book she named the guy "man who was not my husband," sometimes shortening it to "not my husband." Besides that being a mouthful, I don't see the point in disguising it. To me it makes it feel as though it wasn't quite real if there isn't a name attached. So I am saying right now his name was David. Or as he would introduce himself he was "David, as in *Goliath came tumbling down.*"

I did not go out looking for this to happen. I won't deny that David was attractive. He was nearly always smiling and he was vivacious – an ex-theatre kid. He had joined the Army after he got in a bit of trouble with drugs. I don't know if it was the drug use or some innate issue, but I would find out later that he had some mental issues; that man was nuts.

Even though he was an attractive man and we got on well, I never gave a thought to him in *that way*. Not consciously anyway. After this whole ordeal my husband commented that he should have known, because in the majority of my party photos David was dead centre. Maybe subconsciously I was more attracted than I realized.

One night in 2008 I was in a terrible mood. I had a headache. I was annoyed with Dane. I was about to go home, but couldn't be sure if I'd feel better being there anyway. I was alone in the living room while everyone else was out in the kitchen. David came in and asked me what was wrong. I don't remember what I answered. He told me I'd feel better if I had sex with him. I snorted at the thought. Mostly because I thought he was joking – he'd have to be. I didn't feel attractive enough for David, let alone he had never seemed to show that kind of interest in me before. He said he was serious. I told him he'd been drinking, "Talk to me when you're sober" I had said. "We'll discuss it then." But he convinced me to get up and go down town for the St Patricks day events with everyone else.

While everyone was starting to get ready to go, he instructed me to go outside for a cigarette with him. Once the cigarettes were lit, he pulled me by the wrist into the darkness on the side of the house. He wanted me to give him a blow job then and there. It felt reminiscent of my times as a fourteen year old those many years ago. I tried to laugh him off, telling him once again to ask me when he's sober. Just then, one of the females in the group called out to us and then poked her head over the railing of the porch, peering into the darkness. "Oh there you guys are, come on! Let's go!"

"Who's driving?" David said as he gestured at me to follow him. After she was back out of ear shot, he took my face in his hands and whispered in my ear that we'd pick up where we left off later. I don't know why I let him do that or even why I stayed. David could be an aggressive and somewhat domineering man sometimes, but I will explain more about that in another chapter.

As everyone started towards the vehicle, I came out of the house with my purse and David yelled up at me from the driveway. In front of everyone he grinned wide, stretched his arms out sideways, and shouted "Rae! When are you and I going to fuck already?!"

I tried not to show my embarrassment, to pretend he obviously wasn't serious. Everyone laughed. They assumed he was joking. David was a joker. David was exuberant, excessive, and full of life like this on a daily basis. They assumed it was just him being silly, this was just the way he was. David laughed it off as a joke too and as he climbed into the truck he winked at me as if to tell me it was no joke.

Through the night he would whisper something sexual in my ear or grab my ass when no one was looking. I got a little more and then a little more drunk. I was the designated driver, though I probably shouldn't have been.

At the end of the night I drove David's truck back to the house many of them were staying, including David. They were all about to deploy so they had cancelled leases and were all temporarily together. Anyway, David did not get out of the truck. They asked him why he wasn't getting out. He got real serious and said that he and Dane had been having an issue all night and that he wanted me to drive him back there so they could have it out. Friends left, convinced. I had been convinced. But David was still a theatre kid at heart.

"I didn't realize you and Dane were fighting," I said.

"We're not; I just want to get in your pants."

He suddenly grabbed me by the belt in an attempt to pull me towards him or something, but let go when he saw that one of the other guys had come out of the house and was headed back to talk to him. While they were talking I noticed the rosary I had given David hanging from his rear view mirror. This rosary seemed to me a sardonic emblem right at that moment.

After his brief conversation, I drove us back to Dane's house – my car was there anyway. Dane was still up and served up some more drinks. After Dane went to bed and quieted down, David went and double checked. He'd been drinking, but he knew what he was doing. He came back down, got on the couch next to me, grabbed a hold of me and started kissing me. Prompted by something he said, I replied "Well, it doesn't matter. At this point I'm going to hell anyway."

Logically I knew that Jesus died for my sins and blah blah blah... But by then I felt so low about myself. It would take me years to get over this and actually realize the extent of God's grace.

Incidentally, I don't celebrate St Patrick's Day anymore.

ଚ୍ଚଓ

The next morning David called me. We agreed it would be best to pretend it didn't happen, and just be friends until he left for Iraq. But we couldn't just pretend. I saw him a couple of days later at a Dane event. This was a lower key BBQ including people from our church, including our pastor and vicar. David stayed on the other side of the room. We made eye contact, I had to leave. I felt guilty.

I asked Dane to follow me outside. I confessed to him, while not going into much detail. He said he could tell something was wrong between David and me that evening. I could tell he was disappointed in me. I already knew his view point on adulterers. I felt terrible I had betrayed his trust and did what I did in his house.

I internalized. I felt like filth. The whole next week I took to my bed. I was sick to my stomach, literally vomiting, over my own behaviour. I had never felt this way before. I was prone to tears, I slept. All I could do was sleep or I'd feel the pain. I was the most depressed I had ever been in my life. Within the week I told Jason. I could not internalize anymore. Jason was so angry he punched a hole in our wall. I was a bit scared and went to stay with a friend for a few days. I sobbed in Pastor Green's office.

Eventually I went home. I told Jason that maybe it was time to consider divorce. He would have none of that. We fought for a good four hours straight, but in that time he came to realize the toll his behaviour had had on me. Much of it wasn't really his fault, but he hadn't realized how he really came off when he acted the way he did. He came to realize how trapped I had been feeling. It made me cry when he told me that he honestly wasn't surprised that this had happened because he always suspected I was "too good for" him. He always thought I would leave him one day for a better man.

We decided to try to work on the marriage. David was angry that I had told my husband.

೮೦೦೪

A few times over the next couple of weeks David called me out of the blue. He would be drunk. He would tell me things like "Rae, you know we can't be together – it would never work. You are married!" I would respond that I never said I wanted to be with him. The second and third time he called, I would remind him we have already had this conversation.

Finally he called me for the last time. He had decided he was going to pursue a mutual friend and he had not realized that she was quietly engaged to someone else. I had previously mentioned that I thought she was with someone. Well, he had tried to pursue her. She decided to be up front and tell him he had no chance. He called me that day, because in his mind it was my fault. I was apparently standing in the way of his happiness. He went into a rage and started threatening me. I hung up and told my husband.

Jason called him back and told him to stay away from me or he would report him to his superiors. David laughed at him. Jason called his superiors. David had an NCO call Jason to try to smooth things over before the chain of command got notified – but it was too late, it was done.

Dane got involved. Poor guy, but he didn't really realize what was going on. I tried to explain, but David had started using his skill as a liar to sway Dane's opinion. Dane said if David got in trouble he would never speak to me again. I was numb. "Fine then. Bye."

ʃɔɕ

I saw Dane one more time before he deployed, at church. The look of hatred in his eyes was unmistakable. We didn't speak to each other again for two years. At first that was easy enough – he was in Iraq. People at church would ask me how he was. I didn't lie; I just said "I'm not sure, I haven't heard from him in a while." I tried to avoid saying anything that would give it away. Though I was feeling hate, and then indifference, I still had enough of a conscience to not try to tear down his image at church.

A year later he returned. The very first time I saw him, he couldn't hide the surprise in his eyes when he saw my pregnant belly. I'm not sure that I hid my surprise at seeing him either. But we didn't say a word. It went on for about a year, this not speaking. We did not even acknowledge each other's existence. We attended the same church, but we did not see each other. Knowing he was back meant that David was back in town. I was apprehensive I'd run into him, scared of what he would do if I did. Luckily I heard soon after that David had PCS'd to Alaska.

After those two years, I sat in church one day. I had a baby in my arms. Dane was not there, but I don't know that I even noticed by then when he wasn't there. The pastor walked up to the pulpit to discuss prayer requests. Dane was in the ICU at Vanderbilt, in Nashville.

I felt a vice on my heart. My chest tightened. I felt a very real fear that I might lose him before making amends. My first instinct was to drive to Nashville. I stopped myself. The fear of his reaction, of his rejection, stopped me. I convinced myself that if he was still there by a certain day I would make myself go. Luckily, he was released before then.

I had realized how much, deep down, I cared for Dane. We had been friends for a long enough time that I could not just write him off. I emailed him, feeling safer – more shielded – that way. I told him that we weren't children anymore. I told him that whether or not he wanted to consider friendship again, the least we could do was be civilized, act like grown-ups, and acknowledge each other, perhaps even make small talk, at church. I did not receive a reply.

The next Sunday he walked purposefully in my direction. As he passed by he looked me in the eye, he nodded his head, and he said "Hello." It was a start, and I took it.

ಐಐ೪

It was slow going regaining our friendship. We were walking on eggshells. Neither of us really trusted the other. It was a big step of me to introduce him to my daughter.

Shortly after this he deployed again, this time to Afghanistan. This made our transition back to friendship a little easier. We could ease into getting to know each other again with computer screens to shield us. At Christmas time our church would send packages to our members that were deployed. I was given Dane's name.

By the time he came back, I felt comfortable calling him my friend. I was not yet able to start calling him "best friend" again though. We had never even talked about what happened. I still held on to a lot of hurt associated with that. It wasn't until 2013 when I gathered my courage to bring it up. I had thought about it several times, backing down at the last minute. Afraid of another confrontation, afraid he'd be angry. Finally, five years after the fight, we actually talked. He told me he did not realize the extent of what happened with David – of course he didn't, I hadn't been able to explain. He told me his side of the story. He felt guilty. We hashed it out. He also told me that by then he had realized that David was crazy. I don't know the details, but apparently he had gotten married right after getting back and he had treated his wife badly. Dane no longer had anything to do with him. I felt vindicated. It was a releasing conversation and I felt a huge weight fall from my shoulders.

I now call Dane my best friend again.

Chapter 23

"Listen. Slide the weight from your shoulders and move forward. You are afraid you might forget, but you never will. You will forgive and remember."

~Barbara Kingsolver,
The Poisonwood Bible

I would like to describe a little more about the times I had surrounding Dane and David. Until the mistakes and the blow up happened that destroyed friendships, we really did have a good time together.

There were a handful of certain other officers, male and female, that were usually around for the BBQs and parties, but though I liked them all alright I just didn't gain friendships with them really outside of the group activities.

Dane, of course, was my best friend so I saw him all of the time regardless. We often went out to eat together and Dane, even though I call him a chauvinist sometimes, does have a gallant side. At the beginning we would argue over who would pay, I wanted to pay my own way or at least get the bill every other time. Dane would have none of that. He felt, as the man, he should be paying. He also would tell me that if I was picking the restaurant and teaching him about ethnic foods, then it's only fair he'd pay the bill. Ha ha, I still don't know if that argument holds up, especially since we didn't do ethnic restaurants all of the time. He resorted to paying while I was in the bathroom or otherwise distracted. Eventually I learned not to fight him on it, though once in a while I did do my own sneaky paying of the bill. Deep down I appreciated it all, but I just didn't want to feel like I was taking advantage.

We both loved German food, so that is what we ate most often. Our favourite German place being a little bar like establishment in downtown Clarksville on Legion St. It was called Brunie's. It was a bit of a hole in the wall, but I am sad to hear they have closed just recently. Brunie's owner was actually a German woman named, well, "Brunie." I remember the food being excellent. I usually got the Schnitzel with mushroom sauce, German potato salad, and spaetzle... drool... I remember once we were there and as Dane finished his plate Brunie came out to ask how it was and if he wanted more. He said it was delicious and that he was stuffed. She said "Nonsense. You are a growing boy!" She then turned and went to the kitchen to collect another bratwurst to plop on his plate. Dane's eyes got wide, but he did what he was told.

Sometimes after we ate at Brunie's, we would drive over to Silke's Bakery. Silke was also a German lady and her bakery was always so busy. She was a master when it came to breads, pastries, and cakes. She also served lunch items such as pizza and sandwiches. We would go there for dessert, and now I wonder if Silke would ship her amaretto cream cake or her apricot danish internationally... Hmmm.....

We also did many a Sunday lunch at Old Chicago. Dane was working on getting on the "Wall of Foam" multiple times by drinking their whole list of international beers. I lost track of how many times his name was engraved up there, but it was more than once at that location anyway. We would go there on Wednesdays with the group – he more often than I – mainly for the drinking. On Sundays, however; he would usually be in a foul mood and find me at church saying "I need a beer. Meet me at Old Chicago after this." It wasn't always because he was in a foul mood, but I do remember a fair few Sundays I met him there as he drank his beer and listened as he commiserated about something.

Speaking of food; Dane is a grill master. One of the best parts of his parties is that he nearly always got the BBQ out and grilled up some meat. I have never met anyone else that can make any kind of meat like he can. So, so good. When I first started coming along to his house, Dane had no concept of sides. He would serve up just meat and cold beer. It was still really good, but as I became his best friend he started asking me to help him with his parties and I usually became in charge of the sides. I was not responsible, however; for the time that Dane and David ate only plates piled high with sauerkraut. No matter how much I love sauerkraut, I refuse to take responsibility for that.

Often, after a party started to dissipate, Dane would ask me to stay. I wonder if deep down he was more lonely then. I remember one occasion where he had actually gotten angry and basically kicked everyone out, the only time I ever saw him do that. As I went to grab my bag to leave, he stopped me saying "Not you." I would start helping to pick up, sometimes he would say to leave it for later and we would sit down to watch a movie. Usually, he would end up falling asleep half way through in his armchair. I would gently wake him up so he could go to bed. Usually he would be startled out of sleep and say something funny. I would laugh and wonder what he had been dreaming about. I would then send him up to bed and go home myself.

Dane and I would also get together to watch movies or plays that we both liked. My husband never cared for the artsy side of life; especially theatre. Dane appreciated Shakespeare and the like right alongside me, so we made a couple of trips downtown to the Roxy to watch the local productions. I remember seeing at least *Chicago* and *Othello* there with him.

I remember that we actually went with my friend, Laurie, to see one of those. I think it was the *Chicago* one, but I am not sure. She needed to see a production so she could write about it for her theatre class. Laurie was only taking that class as an easy A, though. Dane had not been drinking, so he was not in a jovial mood. Laurie was a bit immature and self-centred at the time. She was a few years younger than us, so that may explain a little of that, but Dane was not in the mood to deal with her.

Laurie would annoy me too sometimes, but that day I remember thinking that Dane was being unreasonable as she was actually acting quite nice. Dane's chauvinistic side started to rear its ugly head as he started to respond to her in a demeaning way. I don't remember what he said, but he insulted her and her feelings were hurt. I stood up for her and punched him in the arm and told him he was being an ass. He cleaned up his behaviour, but I could still tell he wasn't happy with her. I ended up sitting between them at the theatre.

ଽଠଓ

David and I didn't hang out much away from Dane, but there were a few times he'd drop by my job to say hello and chat. I also remember going to lunch with him a couple of times. Once was with Dane, the other was not. If I didn't come to several gatherings in a row, I would eventually receive a message from him asking me where the hell I've been.

As I have mentioned in another chapter, David was an ex-theatre kid. I thought he was so much fun probably because he had that theatre kid quality and we had similar interests. He loved to show off at parties, he loved to sing show tunes.

I also had a chance to see some of his dark side since I had spent enough time with him. I started to notice he was a bit unstable, but it didn't seem to strike me as serious. One part of his personality is that he was very aggressive once he set his eyes on something. He would meet a girl and get very pushy with her if he wanted to have her. I remember the case of Sandi. She was a friend of Laurie's, and I had invited them both over to Dane's one night. This was a pretty casual thing; no other part of the group was there that night – just David, Dane, myself and those two girls. David decided he wanted to take Sandi out. He harassed her the whole night about getting her number, eventually she just gave it to him thinking she'd just avoid him later if she needed to. He insisted that they would be going out on a date and would not take "No" for an answer.

One night we were all going downtown to some local festivities. When we arrived I saw Laurie about to drive away. She told me that Sandi was still there, I knew that David had texted her about coming to meet him and she had replied she had been there and gone home already. I told Laurie that David was here now with the others. Laurie then apparently called Sandi and Sandi cut her night short and left the vicinity. Laurie told me that Sandi was scared of David.

I told David what happened. He did not believe me. I tried to advise him to tone it down with the ladies. Girls he's known for a while may just think its David just being David. But when he was so aggressive from the very first meeting; that could be scary. There are few ladies that want such a domineering man, but even those that do I would imagine wouldn't want to be controlled from the first meeting as I feel David was trying to do. He may not have meant to control her as much as the situation though.

He would sometimes become depressed or angry and Dane would have to talk him down. I remember one time when Dane was not around, David was angry. He stood in the middle of the front yard yelling at God. That in itself is not so crazy, but then he started to have a conversation with God. He was fighting back at God, answering back as if he heard what God was saying. As I sat on the front step, I started to seriously wonder if there really was something wrong with him. That night it was my job to talk him down. That night he directed his anger at me.

ဆဘ

When I had arrived, he was already angry with me. Before I had a chance to get in the door, he grabbed his keys and threw them at me. The keys hit me in the chest and he told me to get in his truck. Instinctively, I bent down to pick the keys up from the front step as he informed me that I would be driving him to get more beer; he had been drinking and didn't want to drive himself. Silently obeying him, I followed him to the truck and got in. Before I even had the chance to start the vehicle he grabbed my hand to stop me turning the key. Clutching my hand tightly, he screamed at me about a perceived offence. I apologized for my minor role in what had upset him – even though I had done nothing wrong. He put his face as close as he could to mine as he snarled at me, the sarcasm dripping, "Oh, you're sorry? You think that makes it alright?!" I apologized repeatedly; I begged him to calm down and told him I knew I was wrong. After what felt like several minutes of berating me, he calmed enough to allow me to drive us to the store. Once there, he commanded me to stay in the vehicle to wait for him.

We arrived back at the house, but David did not want to get out of the truck yet. He was no longer screaming, but he was still upset. We sat in the driveway for several minutes talking; he was not ready to be inside around other people. That's when the police showed up.

The officer gestured for me to roll down the window. He asked us where we had been and what route we had taken. Then he asked us to get out of the truck. Supposedly there had been a hit and run involving a vehicle just like the one we were in. David asked the officer if he knew how many black pickup trucks were in this neighbourhood, let alone Clarksville, TN.

The officer saw the beer on the floorboards and asked if we'd been drinking. David was upfront and said "Yes sir, I have been drinking – but she has not, and she was driving the vehicle." David knew how to switch on his behaviour, even when he was drunk. He knew how to be respectful and hide his inebriation and he displayed this talent for the police officer. I don't think he was ever too drunk to control his behaviour if he wanted to.

The officer alluded to the possibility that we had just switched seats in order to keep David from getting in trouble. Personally, I found this ridiculous. If we had been trying to hide a crime, we would have put the truck in the garage and ran into the house instead of hanging out in the driveway.

I think that possibly he could tell I was on edge and perhaps under duress, so he took me aside while another officer spoke to David and the others that had come out of the house by this point. He said "Look, I can see the officer decal on the truck. I know it's not yours. I know it's his truck. You could get in a lot of trouble for lying for your boyfriend…"

"He's not my boyfriend. He's just a friend." I said as I stared at the ground.

He didn't look as though he believed me, but said "Okay." Then he continued on saying, as he glanced in David's direction, "If you need to come down to the station to speak freely, we can arrange that. You don't have to talk about it with him around. We can protect you."

I scoffed at that. Yeah, right.

The officer told me that the witnesses heard a man and woman arguing in the vehicle in question. David's window had been down when the officer arrived and apparently he had heard the tone of how David was *talking* to me. He asked me one more time if I had anything I needed to report to him. I ignored what I knew he was insinuating.

"Seriously, Officer, I was driving. We didn't see anyone walking on the road, let alone hit them. I am sure I would have realized if I had hit someone."

The police started to inspect the vehicle; they were looking for any sign that it may have been involved in the incident. They pointed to some areas where the finish was smudged – handprints mostly. It seemed to me they were clutching at straws, and I made a mildly sarcastic comment about if David had only kept his truck clean we wouldn't be in this situation. He glared at me and then responded through his clenched teeth fake smile. He was obviously pissed at me and trying not to react in front of the police.

By this point David had called his NCO to come help him out. Even though David himself was an officer, he apparently called the NCO because he didn't want his chain of command to know what was going on. I wonder if this was the same NCO that had tried to call my husband to smooth things over as well.

Eventually, they brought the girl that had been hit – lucky for her she only had minor injuries – and her friend that had been with her. They looked us over from the police cruiser and then told the police officers that it wasn't us that had hit her. That was a relief, but I had been more relieved that David had been yanked out of his aggressive behaviour for the time being.

୫୦୦୫

After this, but prior to his fight with God, he had stormed up to his room, away from everyone else. I apologized for ruining their evening. I had already accepted the guilt that he had placed on me. After a few minutes, he shouted down the stairs "Rae! Get your ass up here!" I was the only one he wanted around him that night, apparently. He turned his music up loud so no one else could hear what was going on. He raged a bit as he continued to drink. Eventually he started to come out of the rage and he passed through stages of calm, depression, reflection – showing me pictures of his family.

After he had his fight with God, he climbed into bed and asked me to stay with him until he fell asleep. I sat on the side of his bed and rubbed his head until he fell asleep as he had asked. Once he was asleep, I kissed him on the forehead and quietly left. Dane had been out of town or something. I told him on the phone the next day. I didn't tell him the details, but Dane said he wished he had been there to talk him down. I had never seen this more extreme behaviour of David's so I wondered if Dane had seen the same kinds of things before. I am sure that David never treated Dane the way he had treated me. Either way, for what it was I think I handled it okay without him, though I had been triggered to act like my fourteen year old self. I also wonder if his now ex-wife, a girl that was occasionally at the gatherings when I wasn't there (I've never met her) had ever seen any of his crazy and if she took it seriously if she did.

Chapter 24

"Please don't take him away from this world. Please don't let him die here in my arms, not after everything we've been through together, not after You've taken so many others. Please, I beg You, let him live."

&Marie Lu,
Champion

Jason and I slowly started trying to pick up and patch our damaged marriage. I quit the drinking and partying. I tried to just be around the house more. Around a month after all of this, it was time for Jason to have his neurosurgery at Vanderbilt Hospital. This was a rough time on the both of us – him more so, obviously. But this ordeal seemed to help our marriage get right back on track.

The surgery was supposed to be relatively straight forward. First a surgery to place an EEG directly on his brain so they could record seizures over a week's time to localize exactly where all the seizures were coming from, then he would have another surgery to remove that piece of the brain.

Things did not go as planned. There was something wrong. I *told* them there was something wrong.

Jason started developing dysphasia, this quickly turned into aphasia. This means he was misusing words. He did not understand why we did not understand him. Then he lost speech all together. This time was pretty scary. Jason's mum had planned to come the next week in time for the second surgery. The first one was not supposed to be that serious. I called her one night when the nurse informed me that the team of doctors were considering the need to move up the second surgery as an emergency. She waited just long enough for Jason's sister Faith to arrive and then they both set out for Tennessee. They arrived shortly before he was in fact sent for emergency surgery. He had had a seizure. One seizure, and it was a bad one.

When he came out from that surgery, it had been successful, but he was still under anaesthesia when they wheeled him into his ICU room. Only one person could stay in the ICU rooms with the patients, so his mum and sister went to leave for the night. Jason woke up. He was enraged. He did not know where he was. Even though he was restrained, he de-intubated himself. He broke his restraints twice. I called his mum, I couldn't deal by myself. Luckily she was still in the hospital. He punched his mother in the

140

stomach; she blocked him and reduced the blow. This young little nurse came in and got too close to his reach. While restrained, he picked her up by the scruff of her neck, her toes barely touching the floor. When she got free, she was visibly scared. She apologized to us, and then ran from the room. Jason was assigned only male nurses from then on out.

All of this was a normal reaction to coming off of the anaesthesia and from waking up after neurosurgery. This information did not make it less scary.

The next day, Jason knew where he was. He could speak. He spoke like a child, but he could speak. We stayed in the hospital for a few more days, his speech and reading slowly getting better. I remember him watching TV. 'Bindi, The Jungle Girl' came on. Jason sounded out *B-in-d-ee*. Then he said "The crocodile man has a daughter called Bindi." I smiled, proud, "That's her!"

৪০৫৪

Later as Jason's thoughts got clearer he told me he couldn't remember anything that happened in the hospital. He said the only thing he remembered was my face and it was crying. He thanked me for staying with him. He also told me he did not feel angry all the time anymore. He did not believe us when we told him about the poor nurse he picked up off of the floor.

Unfortunately, he does not remember Bethany. She was one of his night nurses. He had several good nurses while he was there, but Bethany stood out. She was kind, smart, and effective in her care. She was relatively young, going through a Master's degree at Vanderbilt while working night shifts. I think Jason fancied her a bit. She told him one day that he should clean himself up a bit and brush his teeth. I don't know why no one else had mentioned such a thing, I know I had my mind occupied that it hadn't even crossed my mind, but for a few days no other nurse or CNA had even suggested it. Jason asked if he needed to. She said "Yeah, hun. You stink."

Ha ha. He jumped right up and put on deodorant and brushed his teeth. I don't think he wanted to stink for Nurse Bethany.

Bethany was the one that told me he might be having emergency surgery. The next day, between classes, she came to find me. She came to check on Jason. He was already in surgery by then. She truly cared about her patient.

Because of Nurse Bethany, I decided I wanted to be a nurse.

Chapter 25

"Every atom of your flesh is as dear to me as my own: in pain and sickness it would still be dear."

&Charlotte Brontë,
Jane Eyre

Jason recovered surprisingly fast, especially considering he had had some of the worst reactions in the hospital that the doctors had ever seen. He was supposed to do various therapies for at least eight weeks. After his third meeting they released him and said he was doing so well, he did not have to come back.

I was working at Fort Campbell Federal Credit Union by this point. I became pregnant after just enough time that I was covered by FMLA. This means I could not lose my job for taking time off to have a baby.

We had been trying to have a baby since 2004. I became sick. I wasn't over all feeling bad, but I had diarrhoea for several days and it just wasn't stopping. So during my lunch break one day I went to the doctor's office. The nurse asked me if I could be pregnant. I said no. I had had my period only just before all this started, and no sex since. The nurse left the room and then came back a few minutes later. He said "Guess what? You're pregnant!"

I was very much dehydrated by this time. They hooked me up to an IV and I had to call work and tell them I wasn't coming back because I was there for another six hours. I called Jason. His co-worker picked up at first, apparently Jason had told him I was sick and the guy had teased him that I must be pregnant. When he got on and I told him, he didn't believe me. He thought I was coaxed to tell him that. Eventually I convinced him, although he called me a couple hours later to check on me and ask if I was "still pregnant."

They sent me to the hospital after that to get an ultrasound and a quick look over since I had been so dehydrated. Jason drove out there, but he arrived after they took me back so they didn't let him in. He said he shouldn't have driven because he was shaking the whole way. He said next time tell him news like this when he's safe at home. I have a silly husband.

I had no major issues with my pregnancy, but it was still hard on me. I lost a lot of weight because I threw up every day for two trimesters, I also barely wanted to eat. When I did, I ate masses of fruit. I craved bananas and oranges mostly. I would eat ten pound bags in a day and a half. One day Jason thought he would be clever and took the last two oranges in the sack and carefully peeled them with my citrus peeler. He ate the inside and then carefully folded the peels back up and placed them in the sack. His punishment was that he had to go back to the store to buy me more. I think he thought that his joke was worth it.

The child was sitting on my bowel, restricting my ability to use the facilities. Then in my last trimester I developed gestational diabetes. I was miserable.

One day, a few weeks before my due date, I had an appointment to be induced. I showed up at 5 AM as I was supposed to, got admitted and settled. The nurse came in to induce me. She checked me and then looked at the monitor. She said "Hold on a minute. I need to speak with the doctor," and walked out.

What the hell was wrong with my baby?

Turns out, nothing was wrong. But chick, you need to work on your bedside manner a bit! As it turns out, I was already in labour. I had not even realized. I got my epidural, and the evening of July 24th, 2009 Emma Linnea was born.

ೞೞ

Before Emma had been born I had saved up the money to take the CNA course. My plan was to do CNA first as it was relatively cheap compared to RN school, and I could get my feet wet before I committed to being an RN. All that money ended up going towards baby stuff.

Working at the Credit Union was nice enough, but I was starting to get dissatisfied working in customer service and being yelled at over the phone all the time. I realized that I needed to get started on my dream, not least of all because I wanted to make sure I had something that could support my daughter if – God forbid – anything ever happened to my husband.

I put myself on a strict budget and saved the $1000 in a few months' time. I got into the class and started doing weekend courses. They were eight hour days on Saturday and Sunday, in addition to my Monday thru Friday job. I felt guilty leaving Emma so much, but I knew if I could get this done, I could make it up to her.

Chapter 26

"My mother says healers are born, not made."

๛Suzanne Collins,
The Hunger Games

In 2010, I finally had the means to start working in the medical field, to start on my way to being a nurse. I applied to Vanderbilt. I applied to several jobs at Vanderbilt. Vanderbilt is a big deal of a hospital; a classmate said there was no way I'd get hired as a new CNA. I replied "Well, I won't know until I try." I was determined to work for Vandy. I knew realistically that I might have to accept working somewhere else first for a while, but Vandy was my end goal. Vandy had the doctor that had finally figured out what was wrong with my husband. Vandy had the doctor that fixed my husband. Vandy had Nurse Bethany.

I got a few calls back. I set up interviews with Surgical Step down (9N), Neurology (6N) – Bethany's floor, and a couple others I can't recall. My first interview was on 9N. They asked me why I wanted to work there. I told them a couple reasons, including that it would be a good floor to learn a lot of things on. Then I told them about Jason's surgery. I told them about Nurse Bethany. I told them that if I don't get this job and have to start my career elsewhere, that would be fine but they should rest assured that I intend to end up at Vanderbilt.

I got the job. I cancelled the other interviews, taking the chance while I had it.

A few weeks after I started, I went down to 6N. I did not remember Bethany's last name. I would have sent her a card or something earlier if I had known that sending it to Bethany at Vanderbilt (a hospital of over 20,000 employees) would make it to her. There were four Bethanys on 6N alone. I described her to the staff. They knew who I meant, she was still there they assured me – and told me when she would be back on shift.

The next week I went back to 6N. I asked for Bethany, she heard her name and stood up. It was her. I gave her a hug and told her, as I sobbed, what an effect she had on my life and how I planned to be a nurse like her one day. How much I appreciated all she did for Jason. I still cry when I think about this. After two years, I don't know that she truly remembered me.

She may have, as I have remembered certain patients years after having cared for them, but if she didn't she was gracious enough to pretend that she remembered. I am so glad I had the chance to express my appreciation to her.

හ⃝ශ

9N was a great stepping stone. As expected, I learned a lot of nursing skills and theories while working that floor. I was trained above and beyond the usual CNA skills, reaching close to the level of LPN, but without the accompanying license. I met several lovely nurses that were more than happy to teach what they knew if you were willing to learn. I felt respected and was treated as a peer by most of the RNs. Not all CNAs got that treatment, so I guess I was pretty lucky. Thomas said it was because I was really smart, Naomi said I carried myself like a nurse. It may be because of these two reasons, or it may just be that Thomas liked me – but even Rich treated me like an equal and he was one of the worst for mistreating CNAs.

9N was hard work, but that is not why I transferred from the unit. I had started school by this time, and they would not work with me with my schedule. I knew there were several other units that would work with students, so after nine months I started looking at internal listings.

There was a job on 6C in the Childrens Hospital. 6C was also a critical care unit. It was Paediatric Cardiology. I was unsure if I could handle the emotional side of working with primarily babies that had a relatively high chance of dying. I decided to go for it, I was curious as to if I would like working with kids as it was. I would be contracted to stay a whole year before another transfer would be allowed, but as was common to say at Vandy "You can do anything for a year." I got the job.

I really enjoyed working on 6C, and later 7A after we moved floors. So many young nurses. They were lovely to work with. Sweet girls, mostly Christians – the kind of Christians that really let their light shine if you know what I mean. Once I was talking to one of them and they told me they were Christian. I said "I could tell."

I don't really know that I need to discuss every nurse I worked with there, but I want to record one in the pages of my book. Her name was Viviane. She was young twenties, a perfectly sweet girl. She had started at Vandy as a CNA and worked her way through school until she finally had her RN-BSN. One day, Viviane didn't show up for work. She wasn't there the next day either. It started to trickle around that Viviane had broken her hand and would not be able to work for several weeks. You hear news like this and you are concerned, but only think "Well, that sucks."

Seven weeks later our manager called a meeting. She started off by telling us Viviane would be back the next week. She told us that Viviane wanted us to know. She wanted us to know, because she did not want us to ask questions.

It was true that Viviane broke her hand. But then our manager, Grace, told us something else we did not expect. Something that had not made its way through the gossip line.

"Viviane was beaten by her fiancé."

I still cry when I recall this time.

We learned the details that he beat her in her own apartment. He beat her the day she had found out her father had stage four cancer. He broke her phone so she couldn't call for help. He beat her until he almost killed her. She begged for her life. She begged for him to just let her go. Eventually he did. She had to drive herself to the hospital. She had to drive herself to Baptist Hospital because this piece of shit worked at our emergency department.

He trashed her apartment. She hadn't worked in nearly eight weeks. She didn't have enough PTO to be paid while she was off. So not only did she not have enough for her rent, she also didn't have enough to pay for the damage he had caused. We took up a collection to help her out.

I felt disgusted that I had met this man. I could not believe that someone could be so evil as to do this to one of the sweetest young ladies I had ever met. It would be evil anyway if she hadn't have been a sweet girl – but who? Who could do that to *Viviane*?!

Luckily we worked on a unit that could be locked down. All the Childrens units could be locked down. The front door was always locked, but we were used to having doors between units open. But no more, we couldn't run the risk. He had been suspended from work because of this, who knows what he might try?

I heard he showed up one day when she wasn't there. As far as I know that was the only time. One of my Charge Nurses, Jessica, said one day she didn't know what she would do if he showed up there again. She asked if we thought she'd lose her license if she attacked him.

I said "Well, I saw him strike first. It was self-defence."

Toby said "That's what I saw too."

We were family on 7A.

৪০০৪

Unfortunately while working on this unit, I did know a handful of kids that died. Every one of these children deserves to be remembered, but I don't have the space to add them all into my book. Most of them died at home, or in the ICU. They rarely happened actually on our floor. The whole time a worked there, I only actually saw two deaths. I'd like to tell you about one of them now.

In 2011 I went on maternity leave for four months. On my first night back, I fell right back in the groove – I felt like I had come home.

At the beginning of the night, I got report from the day shift. I was told about a patient that had been there for a while, but she was new to me. She was seventeen. She had a heart condition. She decided that she just didn't want to take her meds anymore. She was embarrassed that she had

151

to when her friends didn't. Her heart stopped. CPR was performed, and she was taken to the ED. They got her heart working, but then she had a stroke. She was nearly brain dead. Her mother signed a DNR/DNI. This means we cannot intervene if she starts to die.

"God, Georgia. Thanks. Giving me a patient that is gonna die on me my first night back!" I made a joke, we laughed. I made a *joke*, and we *laughed*.

It is not unusual for hospital personnel to have a dark sense of humour. You need it sometimes just to get through a shift. If you don't laugh you will cry.

I made a *joke*.

3 AM. A mother's scream.

"Nurse! I need a nurse!"

The alarms hadn't even started ringing yet.

I reached the door at the same time as Emily. Within seconds the alarm started ringing. Emily took the mother by the hands, looked her in the eye. "Do you know what is about to happen?" The mother nodded. "Do you want to change your mind?" The mother said "No," tears already streaming down her face.

Suddenly the monitor went to Asystole. No heartbeat. A big white zero and a long, flat line. This girl took her last breath. No more than two minutes from the mother's first scream, and it was over.

I made a *joke*.

The first thing I thought was "I can't believe I said that to Georgia."

Her sister arrived after hearing the news. She screamed. She screamed for forty-five minutes straight. They couldn't get a hold of her father. It took two hours until his brother had gone to wake him up. The father thought we were all making a fuss. Of course his daughter wasn't dead.

He came brusquely down the hall. He stood in the doorway and snapped her name. He told her to "stop playin'." He went to her bedside and grabbed her arm to shake her. It was ice cold. I saw the realization in his eyes. He dropped to his knees with a yelp. He screamed at the top of his lungs. A few moments later he stumbled towards the hall. He stopped for a moment and turned to look at us at the nurse's station. I will never forget the look on that man's face.

I held it together all morning. Nope, no tears for me. Not until I was safely in my car, with my door shut. Now I was the one screaming. I was raging. I didn't know where these feelings came from. I didn't know her. It was best this way, why was I crying? Why did I cry over this girl, and not the other babies I had known that had passed?

After I calmed down, I was able to reflect. I realized that this was the first death I had ever actually witnessed. That is a powerful enough thing in itself, and I am a doer. We were not allowed to even try to save her. If we had tried and failed, well, alright then. But all I did was stand there and watch her die in her mother's arms.

Chapter 27

"We Vandy! Working hard as we play, this is how we lock it down, yeah how we lock it down! Now we've been made aware; there's some confusion here, so we wrote this jam to point things out and make it crystal clear. There's only one king in this EM game – straight out of Nashville, Tennessee – Vanderbilt is our name! The traumas that we see? They're so ridiculous; we're the only level one in a 150-mile radius. You get hurt on the farm? You get shot in the street? You're coming straight to Vandy, cuz our skills cannot be beat! Now, wait a minute, y'all, I hear one on the roof – intubate and line, he'll be fine – baby it's the truth..."

≈Vanderbilt Emergency Service Resident Physicians 2011,

We Vandy!

Nashville had the Grand Ole Opry, I was fortunate enough to go there twice while in Tennessee. Nashville also had the theatre that Jason took me to see *Wicked!* at as a surprise for our anniversary one year – out of character for him since he doesn't care for the theatre. Nashville had so many restaurants I adored and an awesome artistic community – whether it be music, theatre, or art – but the main draw of Nashville, for me, was Vanderbilt.

Though it was hard work, Vanderbilt has been by and large my favourite place to work. This was largely in part because of some awesome co-workers.

Naomi was my charge nurse on 9N, and she was also one of the few that lived as far out of town as I did. Once we figured that out, we decided to become car pool buddies. There are few people I would care to spend an hour each way in the car with, especially after a twelve hour night shift, but Naomi was a pleasure for me. Our personalities meshed and we just got on well. She respected me above many of the other CNAs, and I learned so much from her – she was wicked smart. She had a take-no-shit, take-no-excuses attitude which rubbed a lot of co-workers the wrong way – but I thought she was wonderful. We also had a lot of laughs together.

We would almost always stop at Starbucks to get fancy coffees before our shift, because she couldn't handle not having the coffee to function and the hospital coffee was straight up gross. I remember once, we were in the drive thru. We made our order, but couldn't move forward because of the line. As she gestured to the menu, she commented that when she sees that she just wants to order everything. I said "Well, when I see it I just want to put my face in the whipped cream and *insert motor-boating imitation here*." To my mortification, we then heard "Uhhh...Okaaay..." and a click from the drive thru speaker as the attendant hung up. I could barely make eye contact with the attendant when we got to the window.

One day, I was driving, and as we came out of the Starbucks parking lot another car cut me off, so I slammed on my brakes. Naomi held her coffee in one hand, and her cigarette in the other. As I hit the brake, she lifted both in the air to steady them. Her body lurched forward and she exclaimed "Ow! My carotid!" I burst out laughing, after she assured herself that her coffee and cigarette were fine, she glared at me. The first thing she did when we got to work was tell everyone in the break room how when I hit the brakes, she hurt herself and I laughed at her pain. I started laughing again. I heard such comments as "Rae, that's mean..."

"No, but you guys don't understand..." I gasped between giggles.

I explained exactly what happened and did the imitation of her saving her coffee and cigarette, along with her very specific injury. Luckily everyone else found it just as funny as I did.

The giggles overtook us more often on the way home when we were delirious with fatigue. Once in a while we would have another RN ride with us that lived about half-way to our destination. One morning when we dropped her off at the Park-and-Ride near her house, I made what was probably the stupidest joke I have ever made – even at the time I knew it wasn't that funny, but I was too tired to stop the thought from coming out of my mouth. The Park-and-Ride is just a parking lot that people park their cars and meet up with others to car pool with. That morning as we pulled up there was a couple that had just parked and were dismounting their bicycles from the back of their car. I said "Huh, they sure are taking *Park-and-Ride* seriously." Both of them started laughing so hard they had tears in their eyes. I was nearly delirious too, but I said "Oh, come on now... that was not *that* funny." They were still laughing, nearly choking. "Stupidest joke I've ever told." I waited a moment. "I give up, y'all are ridiculous. Wake me up when we get home."

ఠఠ

My other favourite 9Ner was Thomas. I did not get to work with him as often, because he did not work every weekend like Naomi and I did, but when he did work my shift it was awesome. He always told me how intelligent I was. That's a nice feeling – to get recognized in a scholarly fashion – especially in a profession like that. I also thought he was very smart, and I loved that he took me under his wing. He would call me into patient rooms, even when they weren't my patients, so that he could show me something interesting or teach me how to do something I likely hadn't seen or done before.

Thomas loved to play on Sporcle to pass the time in the middle of the night. Sporcle was a website that had various types of trivia games in a range of subjects. He always wanted me to play with him. Even when there were several other people gathered around the computer with him, he'd ask "Where's Rae? I need Rae." If I was busy, he'd tell me – or someone to take the message to me – to "Hurry the hell up."

I remember once, playing one of the games that had to do with music. There were very basic clues about what the song was about and you had to guess the name of the song and the artist. There was also a time limit on all of these games. He had another nurse reading out the clues and typing because she was faster at typing and had a better spelling record than he did.

I said "Smack My Bitch Up. Prodigy." They both looked up at me simultaneously, "How... Did you know that?"

They didn't wait for an answer, because we were on a time crunch. She read the next clue.

"Stan. Eminem." I said.

They both looked at me again, this time impressed. "I wouldn't have thought you would know those kinds of songs..." The other nurse said. I shrugged my shoulders at her. I didn't have an answer for that.

Thomas started trying to educate me on his favourite band, Bad Religion, after that. He would also have me attend his smoke breaks, I took smoke breaks myself once in a while and with other people – but even when someone else would be going with him he would still find me and say "Smoke break time! Come on!" He was one of the few that actually noticed that I don't smoke like most other people. I hold cigarettes in between my middle finger and my ring finger, instead of the normal middle and pointer. Naomi noticed that as well, and I think maybe Rich had at one point realized that – though I'm not sure if it was because one of the other two told him. No one else had really paid that much attention to me, I guess.

Thomas was also our resident joker on 9N. There were a handful of other RNs that partook in the fun, and Thomas was often the target since he messed with so many other people. I remember one day someone put lube on the ear piece of a phone and asked me to go tell him there was a phone call for him. I had to feign being bewildered when he cursed. I said "I dunno, Thomas... all I know is that someone told me the Doctor was on that phone for you... I dunno...." He often had me assisting him in his jokes as well – luckily that kept me out of target range.

He was also my favourite breakfast buddy when I was on 9N. On days when I wasn't carpooling, we would walk out together so we could get breakfast on our way out to our cars, as we parked in the same garage. It was a sad day for me when, after I had moved over to Childrens Hospital, I ran into him walking to the garage. He was curt and not his usual friendly self. I asked Naomi what the hell was wrong with him. She said that his fiancé was apparently very jealous and had told him in no uncertain terms to stop talking to certain girls. Naomi was surprised at first he had stopped talking to me, as we had become such good friends, but I suppose that also meant I was a target for the girlfriend to eradicate. I just wish he had said something about it, I would have been bothered – but I would have understood. It still makes me sad that we aren't friends anymore.

ဆဝင

9N was a floor in the adult hospital. We were surgical step-down and trauma overflow. We were the second floor down from the roof, trauma being at the top, so we heard the life flight helicopters landing throughout the night; usually I heard them even as I walked in at ground floor level first thing in the evening. Our hospital had five helipads, including one on the Childrens Hospital roof.

It seems to me that medical professionals that work with adults and trauma are vastly different than the ones that work in paediatrics. On 9N there were a lot more cynical, atheist or agnostic people whereas on 6C I came across many more upbeat Christian personalities.

I remember meeting one nurse, she was fairly new to 9N, she waltzed into the break room and said "What's up, bitches?!" I thought to myself, "I'm going to like her." She and I are still friends, and even though she is an atheist and apparently generally dislikes most Christians (so she alludes to), she has told me before that I am enigma; an educated Christian that doesn't judge. I've told her that I am not an exception to the rule – if she just knew where to look for us, there is more than just me.

I also remember working with a nurse in particular that was a trauma junkie. She would volunteer for every possible nasty wound job that would arise. Like packing an open thoracotomy wound – that one she was excited about. I remember one time we had both just sat down for lunch when we heard over the PA system "STAT 9 NORTH. STAT 9 NORTH." This meant that there was someone in the process of dying on our floor, usually called "coding" in medical terminology. In our hospital a "code" and a "stat" meant the same thing – CPR is about to commence. Kara literally threw her sandwich across the table as she leapt up for action. By the time we got the break room door open, the patient's room was overflowing with people. She found a job not taken yet – the recording – and ducked into the room. Afterwards she was so pleased that she had made it into the room to be amongst the action – and that she got to do a round of CPR.

6C was a different atmosphere. I loved a fair few nurses on 9N, but there were several that were horrible to work with. Nasty to CNAs, and gave me nothing to respect – not only because of their attitudes, but also because in comparing them to others – like all those mentioned in this chapter – they were not nearly as good at their jobs. 6C was also critical care, but most of the nurses there were a lot easier to get along with. At the beginning there were a few that were not very nice, but they were gone before long. Maybe it had to do with working with kids, or maybe it was the kind of illness we were dealing with, but there was a more caring atmosphere and it bled over into the work relationships as well.

We also liked to have fun – there were a lot of laughs on 6C. We would take 10 cc syringes of saline and squirt them at each other from across the hall, or just be all around silly. We liked to have "family lunch" on nightshift, we all tried to be free by 1 or 2 AM to eat our lunch together. This was made even easier when we moved up to 7A where we had a work room in the middle of the unit that was surrounded by windows and had all the monitors in there – so we could easily sit together and still hear patients, and see the monitors. There was a lot more teamwork on this unit as well. A lot more of a "let me help you" attitude instead of the "not my job" attitude that prevailed on 9N.

80C3

There are a few patients from Vanderbilt that I will never forget. Obviously I cannot mention them by name, but I would still like to discuss a couple from each unit.

On 9N, we at one point had a longer term patient, longer than usual. Most patients were in and out of our floor within a week or two tops. This lady had had a whipple surgery. I tell you right now, if a doctor ever tells me I need one of those, I will just say no – I'd rather die naturally. The success rate for those was not very good. Most either got complications immediately, or they would be doing well, go home... and then come back with complications. This patient came back to us after having been home for a while.

To be fair, her complications were not entirely from a failure in the medical procedure. As we came to discover, she had an abusive husband.

160

He had apparently treated her badly her whole life with him. Even her children, I had heard, had their father's attitude towards her. She was supposed to be on a feeding tube. No big deal to hook it up and let the machine run the nutrients directly into her stomach. Her husband decided she did not need that, or that he didn't want to deal with the care of her, and gave her only one breakfast replacement shake a day. Her health deteriorated and she ended up back in the hospital with us. She had severe oedema – weeping oedema in fact. She was so swollen that she could not feel when she went to the bathroom. She was always mortified that she would soil herself and we would have to clean her up. I assured her on many occasions that she did not have to apologize to me. I knew she didn't do it on purpose, besides it was part of my job description – she was just keeping me busy!

I knew she was going to die. Every weekend I would come in surprised to see her name still on the board. She lasted with us for nearly two months. After a while she would start to moan almost constantly. You could hear her in the halls and it would start to grate on some of my co-worker's nerves. Whenever someone would complain, I would snap at them to shut the hell up. She was dying and the moaning was involuntary, but it comforted her somehow.

One day I went in to check on her, she started to cry. She asked me to stay with her for a while. She started saying "Mommy... I don't want to die, Mommy. I don't want to die yet." I knew the end was coming soon. I held her hand and comforted her. When I came out, I predicted to Naomi that she wasn't going to last the week. The next weekend when we came in, her name was erased from the board.

୫୦୧୪

Another patient I won't soon forget was another old lady. The main memorable thing about her is that along with her illness, she also suffered from sundowners. This made nightshifts all the more interesting. Sundowners is an affliction that affects senior citizens, as night falls they basically just start to get confused and this can result in some interesting behaviours. I remember I had this patient with Thomas one night. There were a few minor incidents – like when she unhooked her feeding tube so that we had a nice sticky liquid mess to clean up, or like when she told me the children in the painting in her room were waving to her. She asked us what kind of magic we were doing in this hospital that could make her pictures move – apparently the one in the hall was making faces at her too.

She was such a sweet little lady that I couldn't help but be taken by her. Just the kind of person you want to take care of. She was a fall risk, so we had taken all the precautions we could, including raising the side rails of her bed. I was sitting doing my charting at the nurses station, her room was just off to the side from where I was. I was looking up periodically to check on her when all of a sudden I heard a crash and out of the corner of my eye I saw her head fall level with the floor.

I dropped what I was doing, leaped up and ran for her yelling "Nurse! I need a nurse in here!" Within moments a nurse and another CNA were at my side. I was helping her to sit up, checking her over. She had somehow squeezed between the rails, she told me she just had to go to the bathroom – even though she had a catheter in. "Had" being the operative word – the tube had been caught as she fell. It was pulled all the way out, still inflated at the end with saline – so that's where the blood on the floor came from, that and the IV that had been yanked out of her arm.

We cleaned her up, got her settled again, reattached everything that needed reattaching. I had to get on the Veritas system to do an incident report. One of the nurses commented she had never seen me run so fast as I did when this patient fell. It seems to me that nursing clogs are just made for running. I wore Danskos like many of the RNs and other CNAs and I swear I felt like Wonder Woman running in those. Within the hour her condition worsened and Thomas made the decision that she needed to go to the ICU. I do not know what the outcome was for her after that, unfortunately.

৪০৫৪

Paediatric Cardiology has a handful of kids I remember. Many of our kids were long term or reoccurring patients due entirely to the nature of their illness and of the nature of the surgeries they required.

I am going to tell you about two different boys that I remember. These are two that touched me in some way – even though I tried to keep my distance from getting attached to these kids.

The first one was a baby that had been with us since he was born. He was there for the first eight months of his life before he was finally allowed to go home for a while. His condition – Hypoplastic Left Heart Syndrome – meant that he would need three major surgeries by the time he was three years old. The first two being within his first couple months of his life. When he was finally stable after the second one (a struggle for these babies, if they die it is usually within this period), he got to go home to live and just have frequent clinic visits until he was about three and could come back for his last surgery. Many of these kids also required complete heart transplants later in life, but that was not the obviously necessary step upon diagnosis of this condition.

His parents, especially his mum, always rubbed me the wrong way anyway. It's easy enough to say after the fact, I know, but I literally would time my vitals checks for him around when she would be out of the room. She was just plain hateful.

This boy went home. His parents decided it was too much trouble to keep giving him his meds after a while. Excuses abounded about the pharmacy the script was at was too far, and they had to order it ahead of time. The clinic visits were a pain because they were so far away and so frequent as well. They stopped taking him to his appointments.

By the time we knew anything about it, he was a year and a half. His heart had stopped; his grandfather happened to be with him and performed CPR. He got him to their local emergency department where he was revived and then life flighted to us.

After his condition was assessed by the team of doctors, they realized his heart was so damaged that it was no longer a viable option to have his third surgery. "The only thing that might save him now" they said "would be a heart transplant." The thing was... the way his parents had treated his heart made him ineligible to get a new heart. They had the gall to threaten to sue the hospital. Of all the nerve, these people... I can't even.

To top it off, the mother was twelve weeks pregnant by this point. The doctors advised her to go get her check-ups. She already had a baby with a congenital heart defect; she was at high risk of having another if she didn't properly take care of her pregnancy. The whole month they were with us, she never saw a doctor for herself, and she continued to have frequent smoke breaks.

I raged about it on my way home one day. How. Dare. She. How dare they?! He fought so hard for his life, and then you – you who should have taken care of him – you did this.

Naturally I was upset that this baby was going to die, but I understood the hospital's standpoint. I knew that hearts are hard to come by, and if one came along it would be best to go to someone that would at least try to take care of it.

Eventually he went home. We heard within a couple weeks that he had passed. Sweet angel boy, I mourn your passing still.

ಶೋಚ

One of my favourite songs at this time was from The Band Perry. It was called "If I Die Young." How fitting for someone working with critically ill children.

December 2011 was an especially hard month for 7A. There was an unusually high amount of deaths of our kids. Not all with us, some kids we never heard updates from – others we would get reports that they died at home, in the ED, or in the PCICU. I was on maternity leave still at this time, so I was shielded more than my co-workers were.

I did find out, however; about one boy. He was a little ball of sass. I tried to keep myself unattached, but there was just something about this little ray of sunshine. He was four years old, a frequent flier with us. He would get so excited when I wore my Spiderman scrubs, Spiderman was his favourite and we often called him that as his nickname. He had come back and ended up staying this time for several months. When I left for leave, I just assumed I'd see him when I got back. He was sick enough to be with us, but not so sick that I saw death coming.

Over the next couple months his condition worsened, he needed a new heart. He was at the top of the list, but one just wasn't available. My co-workers saw the deterioration. They had the chance to hug him and tell him goodbye. I saw pictures and video later of him from close to his time and I knew if I had been there to see it beforehand, the news would not have come as a shock.

I found out that he had died in the PCICU the day before his fifth birthday. The day I found out I was travelling to my in laws for Christmas. I got behind the wheel of my car and turned on "If I Die Young." I listened to it over and over, tears running down my face.

Chapter 28

"...and she loved a little boy very, very much – even more than she loved herself."

&Shel Silverstein,
The Giving Tree

While at Vandy, I accidentally got pregnant again. We had planned on having another baby eventually, but I had wanted to finish school first. Luckily I was once again eligible for FMLA.

The pregnancy with Levi was a lot easier on me. I did not throw up once, and I had a fair appetite. Jason was so sure we were going to have another girl. I told him I felt different, I was sure it was a boy. He refused to waste time talking about boy names. When I found out for sure it was a boy, I called him to gloat. He said "Man! Now I have to start my list all over again!"

I worked the entire time I was pregnant. I was actually scheduled for another week when I went into the doctor's office for a check-up.

The doctor's office building was attached to the hospital by a long corridor. During my check-up, the doctor furrowed his brow and said the baby's heart beat was a lot slower than usual. He wanted me to walk over to the hospital and admit myself. He wanted to monitor the baby. He did not tell me that baby heart rates slow when there are contractions. He assumed I knew that. I walked down that corridor. I called Jason, I was crying and I was scared.

Once I was settled the nurse assured me there was nothing to fear. After a couple hours the doctor came and told me I was in labour. I hadn't realized this time either. I called my boss to cancel my schedule, I called my Medical Microbiology professor to tell her I wouldn't be there that night, and then I called Jason's mum. She had been planning on coming in a couple weeks to be with Emma while I was in hospital. She dropped everything and drove the six hours to Clarksville. Jason brought Emma to the hospital, and his mum arrived just as he took her into the hall because I was starting to push. This allowed Jason to make it back into the room. The timing could not have been more perfect.

Levi Isaac was born the evening of September 7, 2011.

By the time I had Levi, I had been back at College for nearly a year and a half. I was doing a full course load, half on location, half online. I was working hard and making all As and Bs, studying and doing class work while Emma was in day care, working mostly night shift on the weekends at Vandy to be able to afford school.

When I found out I would be having a baby in the autumn of 2011, I lessened my course load just for that semester. I worked ahead as much as possible for the online courses, so I was effectively done with them by the time Levi arrived. I missed only two Medical Microbiology classes, much to my professor's amazement. She made me sit in a comfy chair when I arrived back.

That next year I actually acquired two associate degrees: one Associate of Science, and one accidental Associate of Arts. I graduated with honours after being offered a membership with Phi Theta Kappa – the honours society. I had started applying to RN schools, now that I had all the pre-reqs out of the way. I took a few entrance exams, for the program at my current school the examiner said I had gotten the highest score she had ever seen. I got in to that program. I applied to only one other nursing school. I applied on the off chance I might get a place in their online program. I thought that may ease up my schedule just a bit. They accepted over sixty students a semester into their regular RN program, but their online program was much more competitive. They only accepted fifteen to twenty a semester there. I got into the online program.

Shortly after gaining my acceptances, Jason came to me with news. He had applied for a transfer. He had been trying to hold off till I was done school, but he really disliked where he was at. He applied to this job not believing he would actually get it. He applied because he thought I'd be pleased if he did get it. I was a little concerned for my schooling, and bummed that I wouldn't get to do the program with my good friend, Nicki... But what the hell?! I had always loved Australia!

Chapter 29

"Life is a book and there are a thousand pages I have not yet read."

&Cassandra Clare,
Clockwork Princess

It took a while to actually get out to Australia. There was a lot of paperwork and things we had to wait on from the government before we could go. We were given an estimate that we would be there in September of 2012, so I gave a month's notice and quit work by August. I wish I hadn't have done that so early, I really enjoyed my job and the experience was invaluable. As it turned out, from various hold ups including a hurricane that temporarily closed the government office handling Jason's clearance, we did not actually arrive in Alice Springs until February 1st, 2013.

A cross continental trip is stressful enough without kids, but I had a one year old and a three year old with me. Even though they were actually pretty well behaved, I would not do that trip again if I didn't have to until I had kids that could at least walk and carry their own bags.

We arrived to a house devoid of food. We were exhausted. We were hungry. Sigh, we had to go to the grocery store. I remember Levi crying and laying his head on the handle of the trolley, eventually falling asleep. Poor bud, all he wanted to do was sleep and I couldn't blame him. As we came out of the grocery store, I heard someone shout my name. I turned and saw Tisha – a girl I had gone to school with in Alice twenty years before! What are the odds, I wonder?

Since our sponsor was so ill equipped to help a new family at that time (he was working shift work and his wife was away for an extended trip. He was also only told we were arriving a couple of days before we got there.) I was lucky to already have a few friends around town still. One person that took me under her wing was my old best friend, Jennifer's, mum Toni. Jennifer was no longer here, but her parents and youngest sister had moved back. One week after arriving, on my birthday, Toni took the kids and me to her women's Bible study at an evangelical church. This church was now called "Desert Life," but it was actually the same church I had attended twenty years before – when it was called "Community Church."

I wasn't so sure I wanted to overall become involved in that kind of church again, but I wanted to make myself get up and start meeting people so that I wouldn't feel isolated and fall into a depression. I met several lovely ladies there, including a good handful of Americans, and they accepted me in and made me feel welcome. They had a kids program at the same time where Emma and Levi could go, play, do a craft, and learn about Jesus. I don't always agree with specific theology, but I do still attend after a year and a half, and Nourish ladies Bible study is a big part of my week.

We decided to start our church-home hunt after we got settled. Jason has not been much of a church goer, but he went with me anyway. We tried Desert Life first, because I felt obligated to at least try it since I was attending the Bible study. Jason is more of a traditionalist and did not like the loud music and the charismatic evangelical style. We crossed it off of our list.

Next we tried the Lutheran church, because, well... I'm Lutheran. Jason is not Lutheran, but at least it is generally a more traditional style church and he appreciates that. We did not feel comfortable there, and then I started to hear rumours about some strange theology that had been preached there in the past. We crossed it off the list.

Next we went to the Anglican church. We liked it; it was close enough to a Lutheran service that I felt comfortable, and traditional style enough that Jason felt comfortable. They did not, however; have any provisions for young children attending there. During the school year they had Sunday school during the service for grade five and above – but nothing, not even a quiet room, for babies and toddlers. I thought that was a bit backward. After several Sundays I finally decided to look again to see if we could find a better fit. I tried the Baptist church; Jason refused to try the Catholic church. Eventually I made my way back to Desert Life. They had a great kids program, and Emma loved Sunday school there. So that's where I ended up.

At least now, as an adult, I feel much more accepted in that environment. I actually met one lady once that exclaimed "Oh, you're Rae! I've heard so many good things about you from the Nourish ladies – they talk about you all the time!"

"Really?" I asked.

"Yes," she said, "They are forever talking about what a wonderful woman of God you are."

I thought that must be a first. I'm rarely, if ever, discussed at length as a good Christian woman among 'Church-People.' I thought if this was the case, maybe I should stick it out with Desert Life for a while longer.

೮೦೧೩

I had some plans, big plans, for my nursing career. Unfortunately my carefully laid plans usually seem to get derailed. I forever have to revaluate and change course. By now, I had decided to finish an RN degree at CDU in Alice Springs, and then if we stayed long enough, perhaps bridge to their midwifery program.

I was told before I went that CDU had a deal with the company my husband worked for so that American spouses could get the local tuition rate. They tried to charge me $20,000 a year for being an International student. I gave them my tuition waiver letter. They told me that the deal had been cancelled the previous year, citing some government tuition act. Personally, I read it and I did not see how it applied. I tried to argue with them, they showed me letters and responses to and from the CLO officer from where my husband worked. She had sent a letter on behalf of someone else and had laid down the argument after one response. What really made me angry though was that I had told her to her face what my plans were. I had discussed the tuition waiver letter with her – and she never mentioned to me that it was a no longer viable option. Apparently, she hadn't told anyone else that should have known either.

I cried. I couldn't afford $20,000 a year. I couldn't get FAFSA aid for an Aussie school. I couldn't get Aussie scholarships because I was American. I couldn't do RN completely online in the US either – it's something that has to have clinicals and check offs occasionally. I cried, and I cried, and then I came up with a new plan.

I had started volunteering with St John Ambulance. It was a place that I could keep up with some medical skills, and get a taste of emergency medicine. I decided to throw myself even more into it. If nothing else, it would look good on my resume for later. After a bit I started working primarily with the cadet program. A program that kids aged eight to eighteen come for meetings, earn badges, and learn first aid. The senior cadets also getting to go out on duties with adult volunteers to help and gain more skills. It is a wonderful program, and I had wished that I had known it existed when I lived here before.

I started doing some admin work to help the Superintendent out, then six or so months later I was promoted to a Divisional Officer role. Still under this role I was doing a lot of Admin work, but I also started doing a lot more direct teaching of the cadets. Five months later I was promoted again. This time to Superintendent, as the previous one had been promoted to a Territory position. This would definitely look good on a resume.

Earlier this same year a job kind of fell in my lap. It was perfect. It was a PCA job, which is similar to what we called CNA in the States. I had looked a bit for a job when I first moved, but everything I was offered did not pay enough to cover the enormous cost of day care for two children that they charge here. I had decided to take advantage of the chance to not have to work and spend more time with my kids while they were young. This PCA job, however; paid well and was a casual position. I only worked when I wanted to. I could spare time for my kids, make a little money, and better yet – get more experience under my belt. I worked with mental health patients, I don't think that is a path I want to end up in, but I've long had the view that I should experience a bit of every kind of nursing if I can, especially before deciding what to specialize in.

Within six months I saw a listing for a job called "PCA Supervisor" at the Alice Springs Hospital. I applied. The opportunity was too good to pass up

— this job would include management duties, as well as overseeing the Hospital's 70+ PCA workforce in terms of their training, development, and compliance. Since I someday plan to become either a Nurse Manager or a Nurse Educator, this would be perfect experience. I thought I was going in for an interview. Turns out I was offered the job on the spot and the role was explained to me and asked if I had any questions. It turned out the director had interviewed me a year before, found me suitable, but I backed out when I realized I wouldn't be able to afford child care. He remembered me, and didn't feel the need to interview me again it seems. Now my daughter is about to start school, so my child care costs are not as significant (though still not cheap!) But I can afford to take the opportunity.

Chapter 30

"I know of no fine words to do with love. They wither like flowers when I try to pick them."

୫*Dina*
I am Dina

I fear as the years go on, and as my emotions are often guarded, that my husband doesn't quite understand how much we – I – really do love him. I am working on telling him more often, even tougher is me working on showing him.

Throughout the years, I have periodically tried to do nice things or give him a spontaneous kiss to try to express myself and usually he looks at me as if I've grown two heads because it is out of character for me. It's like he expects that I am just trying to get something out of him.

One night, I worked hard to put together a "52 reasons I love you" booklet made out of playing cards. It was an idea I got off of the internet. He seemed to appreciate it, but I would hope that he would realize that I was sincere and be able to flip through it whenever he might question how I really feel. I don't think he does, though.

Our relationship certainly has had a rocky past. We don't have a whole lot of similar hobbies. We don't always see eye to eye, or view the same circumstances or facts with the same viewpoint. I don't know if that has to do strictly with our different personalities or the fact that one of us is female and the other male. I think that I am being plain and honest, and yet sometimes he reads into something with a view that I did not intend. Stories that display what I think are cute behaviours, he may think make him look foolish or unmanly. I don't intend for him to feel that way.

I am going to make this chapter about my husband, so that I can attempt to express my feelings about him without other stories overshadowing the part he plays in my life.

Jason is a man that loves his family. I am proud to say that he is a man that wanted his children and I never had to worry whether he would be a deadbeat dad. He was nervous and shaking when he found out I was pregnant, he worried over me while I was pregnant – calling his mum, telling her he was worried that I was losing so much weight, that I was barely eating except for my fruit, he spoke in hushed tones, I assume so I wouldn't hear.

When the time came to have Emma, he stayed faithfully by my side. He was visibly nervous, as he walked back and forth, wanting to catch a glimpse of her as she came out and then getting out of the Doctor's way to come back and gently stroke my arm or my hair. He had a look of wonder as he held her for the first time; I wanted to cry at how sweet the scene was.

He adored his daughter from the start, he was a champ helping to take care of her while I was going through CNA school, and then later when I started to work at the hospital. He was happy enough when I got pregnant again, thinking we'd have another girl, then there was his excitement when he found out he was going to have a son.

Shortly after our son was born, Jason took me to see *Wicked!* on stage in Nashville. I've mentioned that this was out of character for him, as things like this are not in his lists of interests, but I had a wonderful time and got to educate him a bit on theatre etiquette. I know he wasn't as impressed as I was with the production, but I hoped that he realized that I had a really good time and that I thoroughly appreciated him doing that for me as a belated anniversary gift.

I appreciate that my husband works hard to take care of me and my kids, I appreciate that he is a good man with high values. He has an old school viewpoint, and sometimes I struggle to fit into the role of the kind of wife he expects me to be. When I struggle or fail in this area, I think he thinks that I must not appreciate his efforts or that I must not really care or really love him. He puts up with a lot of crap from me, I know it.

I appreciate that he took care of the kids a lot while I was working weekends and nightshifts, I appreciate that he supported me through school thus far. I appreciate that he applied for a job in Alice Springs, Australia just because he knew I would be pleased if he got it.

I appreciate that he got dressed up and attended his children's infant baptisms at my Lutheran Church, even though he doesn't believe in it, because it was important to me. I appreciate that when he gets me gifts for whatever occasions, he obviously tries hard to give me something he knows I'd like.

I know full well that I hit a jackpot when I married my husband. He takes care of me, he has a good job, he is responsible, I have nice in laws, and he makes beautiful babies. I also suspect, deep down, he loves me too – though I don't know why sometimes.

He thinks I never defended him to my mum when they went through a period of not liking each other – but in our first year of marriage my mum would often tell me I didn't have to stay married to him if I didn't want to. This was unwarranted "advice," and I told her every single time that I loved Jason and that there was nothing wrong in our relationship. Finally I informed her that if she said one more negative thing about my husband, I would never speak to her again.

He has forgiven me for not being there enough when he was struggling with his health issue, for my behaviour during that time – when I was hiding behind alcohol... and when I did other horrid things related to that time. He did not divorce me at my lowest.

Sometimes I assume that he just knows I love and appreciate him. After all, I am still around, aren't I? I assume he understands that when I make him food or a drink he didn't ask for, or give him little no-occasion gifts that these are tokens of my love. I assumed he understood that I thought he liked it when I would take kids out of the house occasionally on his days off so he could have time to himself – to sleep, to watch his shows. Apparently I was wrong, and he viewed it as us not wanting to spend time with him.

Jason Meadows, I love you. Your kids love you. You are a good daddy and we really do appreciate all you do for us.

Chapter 31

"He lingered at the door, and said, 'The Lion wants courage, the Tin Man a heart, and the Scarecrow brains. Dorothy wants to go home. What do you want?'...
She couldn't say forgiveness, not to Liir. She started to say 'a soldier,' to make fun of his mooning affections over the guys in uniform. But realizing even as she said it that he would be hurt, she caught herself halfway, and in the end what came out of her mouth surprised them both.
She said, 'A soul-'
He blinked at her."

∞Gregory Maguire,
Wicked: The Life and Times of the Wicked Witch of the West

I was sitting in my car in the church parking lot. I had come for a women's conference, but I was early. I sat, feeling raw from the events those previous weeks.

I had started to write an autobiography – a memoir if you will. When I got to the chapter about Wyatt, I had just let it all pour out of me; a private release on paper. Though silent tears poured as I wrote it, I felt exuberance as I finished. I felt joy for the first time in relation to him.

The next week, I was preparing a lesson plan for a group of youth I work with. This particular lesson coincided with National Child Protection week, so our topics had to do with various youth issues relating to their personal protection; bullying, drug and alcohol abuse, depression/suicide... and dating abuse.

I had felt such a release and I thought "Well, it has been sixteen years – I'm over it." So I decided to go ahead and relate my own dating abuse story to these kids. I thought my experience could serve as a relatable resource for them.

If any of them happened to be dealing with something similar then they would know Ms Rae could understand and would be in their corner.

In the meantime, as I prepared the lesson, I had sent some partial manuscripts to three of my long time best friends to read and review for me. I got a response from all three that I had not expected.

"Honestly, Rae, I had an idea that you had a bad relationship before we met – but, you know, you've never actually told me about it before."

And "I had a feeling that you may have had an abusive boyfriend before – but you never said anything about it."

The responses came as a surprise to me. I suddenly realized that if I hadn't told them about it, then I must not have ever told anyone. I met Svea as my relationship with Wyatt was drawing to a close, I met Maja a year or so later. If I hadn't told them in the sixteen and fifteen years, respectively – and I hadn't told Dane in the eight years I've known him – then I hadn't told anyone. I suddenly realized that not even my husband knew yet.

I went to do a rewrite of my story, just to make sure it was appropriate to my youth audience. I realized that my first draft had made excuses for him and I realized that this was not okay. I realized if I was going to tell the story for the benefit of others, I was doing a disservice to them – and myself – if I made excuses and did not tell the whole truth. I sat down and I lived it again.

A fear welled up inside me as the day drew nearer to tell this story *out loud*. It was one thing to release it on paper, but quite another to speak it out I realized. I knew if I were to tell these kids, I would need to tell my husband finally as well. I was even more nervous about this.

I was such a chicken about it that I just printed it out and as I was on my way out the door, I took a deep breath and said "Jason, did I ever tell you about my abusive ex?" Secretly hoping maybe I had.

"No." He said; a confused look on his face.

My eyes averted from his gaze. I said "Well, I am teaching a module on dating abuse tonight and I'm about to tell my cadets about it... So, uh... please read this... and I'm not going to want to talk about it."

I then rushed myself out the door. I felt like an idiot, a jerk, like I had any number of negative personality disorders.

Overall, the lesson went well. The cadets were attentive and respectful. However; in speaking it out loud I had released a whole new wave of emotions.

By the time I was sitting in that church parking lot, I felt raw. I have long been a conservative, reserved soul. When I was a youth, I went to a contemporary church like this one; but even then I was never comfortable displaying devotion. I was uncomfortable closing my eyes and raising my hands in service. I have long been uncomfortable with charismatics and Pentecostal "speaking in tongues." Then I had become a conservative WELS Lutheran and was definitely further removed from these behaviours.

Regardless, I sat outside of this contemporary church I had been attending. I decided to go inside, early though I was, hoping to find one of my friends to chat with. Everyone was busy with set up and the worship team was practicing, so I sat in the last row to listen.

Before I knew what was happening, big fat tears were rolling down my face. I realized that I still wasn't over it. Even sixteen years and getting it off of my chest had not cleared the feelings I had kept locked inside.

A couple of friends checked on me and brought me tissues. Eventually I composed myself enough before the conference started.

The speaker that night told of the woman who bled for twelve years. She said:

"I have no doubt in this room with this many of us, that some of us have felt those reasons as well; reasons to feel ashamed, reasons to feel rejected, reasons to feel isolated. Seasons when we have felt alone, seasons when we have felt bitter or resentment... This woman spent twelve years suffering... She was considered "Unclean" and she probably would have felt a lot of shame... *Maybe some of you have carried something for twelve years* whether it is a medical condition, a broken heart, *a wound somewhere in your soul... Maybe you've carried around something that long and maybe you know over time it does deplete you, wears you down and you get to a point where you feel hopeless.* But you know what? This woman decided that she had had enough... Jesus knew she needed more than healing; she needed wholeness... She told him the whole truth – *it may have been the first time in her life she had been able to speak those words.* He took away her shame, validated her and called her daughter."

Somehow this just hit me to the core. Twelve years? More like sixteen years in my case, but close enough. It is a truly amazing feeling when you go to church and the sermon seems to be cherry picked just for you. You wonder "How did she know?"

She did an altar call; calling for people that needed healing of some sort. She seemed to be speaking directly to me. But I am not the kind that gets up for altar calls. They make me uncomfortable.

She said "I'd love to pray for girls tonight. I'd love to stand and pray for any of you, that like this woman needs to be made whole. Whether it's one woman or a hundred... He already knows who this word is for and who needs this healing, so if we're hesitating in our hearts, it's only us we're fooling."

I felt a tug, like strings pulling my chest forward. My feet started to move and I found myself at the altar.

A friend came up behind me and laid her hand on my shoulder. As she started to pray, the tears started again. Within moments my knees gave way – I was on the ground, sobbing. I curled up in a ball and buried my face in my arms.

ಬಂಛ

I wanted my daughter to know. I wanted my son to see. I wrote a book and in it I revealed a story of abuse.

I hadn't spoken about it to Dane; I hadn't spoken about it to Svea and Maja. I hadn't spoken, because honestly I still feel the after effects of that relationship. In searching my soul, I have come to recognize how my relationship with him has affected many of my subsequent relationships. I have made poor choices. Anyone clouded by love – especially young love – is bound to make at least a few poor choices, but the ones I regret the most I find have that relationship as their source.

My first boyfriend moulded my brain when it was still young enough, still growing and making connections. Sixteen years later, whenever there is an issue in my relationship, my first thoughts are not healthy ones. Even with a caring partner, my first thought will take the abusive route first. That is what my head expects, and I have to push the thoughts back out again. My head will tell me that I am not good enough or that I would deserve whatever retribution it would initially expect. When Dane and I had our big blowout, my first thought was that it would have been easier to take if he had just slapped me in the face.

I have largely overcome these obstacles, I learned over the years to push those feelings back down. I learned, I forced myself, to be bold and assertive. I used my passion for theatre to hide and pretend that I was somebody I wasn't, a perfect way to work through certain issues. I have also put guards up, which I know affect my behaviour and can baffle my husband sometimes.

I remember being intimidated by Danny, and having to make myself be bold. I remember standing in Sven's embrace, clenching my fist and willing myself not to run from something that scares me – because I could not be assertive and I was afraid of ruining his night. I remember David throwing his keys at me and my apologizing even when I had done nothing wrong. I remember the feeling of worthlessness becoming so overwhelming at times. Feeling worthless because I didn't think any guy really liked me or wanted me.

I battled clinical depression as a youth; I turned to alcohol to numb my pain as an adult. I let myself become so worthless in my own eyes that I did what I did with David.

I also realize that I became best friends with a chauvinist. A sweet guy, but a proud chauvinist nonetheless. What kind of self-respecting woman nowadays does that? I am glad to say he has grown significantly in the past eight years I have known him, and his behaviour towards women has significantly improved. He used to have much more of a misogynistic outlook, if I'm honest. What kind of state was I in when I met him, that I thought his views towards women were normal?

I have two beautiful redheaded children; they are beautiful inside and out. I can already see myself in my daughter, and that scares me. She is beautiful, I know she will be a heart breaker when she grows up – yet I also know, kids can be mean and life can be hard. I know that no matter how pretty your Momma might think you are there is still room for insecurities to grow.

I'm afraid she'll meet a boy that wants to control her. I'm afraid she'll go to parties as a teenager where all the boys pay attention to other girls, and that this will make her question her attractiveness. I'm afraid that she will meet a boy that she cares for that will make her question her worth. I'm afraid she will have sex as a teenager... I know I did it, so I can't talk... but dang-it, I'm the mum and I can't bear to think of men doing to her what they did to me *shudder.* I'm afraid that when she does do it, she won't be ready.

I'm afraid that both my children will meet some questionable "Christians" that will judge them and threaten their relationship with God. I have many fears when it comes to my children, but I also have high hopes for them. I hope they both grow up to be wonderful people of God. I hope that they both find someone they love and who loves them unconditionally. I hope they give me equally beautiful grandchildren someday.

I hope that knowing me and my story, they will learn from my mistakes and they will appreciate their heritage. I hope my eventual grandchildren will benefit from me as well.

I hope that I can make my children understand God's grace. Grace is a tricky word; many Christians throw it around and don't really know the deeper meaning of it. In the definition as is associated with Christ, grace means "unmerited favour." This means that we are getting what we *don't* deserve. I deserve so much retribution and judgement for things like the incident with David, but through God's unmerited favour He has forgiven me. It took a long while for me to heal from the guilt of David. Every year around that time I would go into a depression, the depression getting slightly less each year as time started to heal my wounds. It wasn't until this year, 2014, that I really realized the implications of God's forgiveness, mercy, and grace. Jesus died for my sins – He died for everyone's sins; even the sins of those who do not believe. I hope that my children also will come to understand that even if there are people whose lifestyle or religion they do not agree with; God's grace is sufficient for everyone and through His grace we are to show grace and love to others.

৯০৫৪

I sat down in front of my laptop one Saturday night in 2014. As I logged on, I wondered if I wrote a book, would anyone read it?

Made in the USA
Charleston, SC
11 April 2015